FARE WELL IN CHRIST

FARE WELL IN CHRIST

W. H. Vanstone

DARTON·LONGMAN+TODD

First published in 1997 by
Darton, Longman and Todd Ltd
1 Spencer Court
140–142 Wandsworth High Street
London SW18 4JJ

Reprinted 1998

ISBN 0–232–52220–0

A catalogue record for this book is available
from the British Library

Designed by Sandie Boccacci

Phototypeset in 10/14.25 pt Adobe Caslon by Intype London Ltd
Printed and bound in Great Britain by
Page Bros, Norwich

To David and Helen Wyatt
quorum exemplum necnon et amicitia
per multos annos
lux mihi gratissima
H. D. L.

CONTENTS

FOREWORD

THOSE OF US who are old are sometimes accused by the young of 'living in the past'. Certainly we talk about the past more than the young do: our memories contain more of the past than do theirs. But to remember and refer to the past is not necessarily 'to live in the past'; very often to recall the past is to enrich the present. In old age we continue to use our brains: ideas and possibilities continue to occur to us and our brains continue to examine them and ponder over them.

But I find that in old age my brain works ever more slowly. It does not flow like a torrent or race like a swift: it *grinds* along. So it takes me an awfully long time to put together a few ideas and possibilities in a reasonably coherent way. The progress of this book has been 'grinding along' for nearly five years, and it would never have reached completion but for the kindness and constant encouragement of my dear friends Ted and Ruth Kelly and the services of their magic word processor in transforming my barely legible manuscript into a form which might be acceptable to a publisher.

W. H. VANSTONE

Chapter One

THE GRACE OF GOD

I N THE COURSE OF my ministry as a priest there was a period of fifteen years when I had no occasion or opportunity to preach a sermon on Christmas Day. When an occasion eventually came my way it was to be at a church where the Alternative Service Book of the Church of England had already come into regular use; and this book, of course, allows to priests a degree of choice among the passages of Scripture which may be read at the Eucharist on Christmas Day and upon which the priest may base the homily or sermon. Naturally, therefore, I looked rather carefully at these passages among which I was to find the basis or theme or text for my Christmas sermon.

I was immediately impressed by the opening sentence of a passage from the Epistle to Titus: 'The grace of God has dawned upon the world with healing for all mankind.' It seemed a succinct and very beautiful expression of the meaning of Christmas and one which would not be so familiar to the congregation as to be taken as a mere platitude. The word 'dawned' seemed particularly appropriate: for, while it is a perfectly legitimate translation of the original Greek word, it has associations and evocations which would be lacking if we read that the grace of God has 'come into' or 'arrived' or 'appeared' in the world. We use the word 'dawned' metaphorically only of some new thing which is welcome to mankind and brings good hope and expectation: we speak of the dawn of civilisation or the dawn of the Renaissance or the dawn of the peace-process, but we never speak of the dawn of a war or of a new disease or of a great famine. Anything which 'dawns' upon us is, almost by definition, welcome and attractive to us and a ground of good hope. Dawn is the harbinger and herald of the coming of light – the 'gladdening light', the 'kindly light' – which enables us human beings to make effective use of our eyes and gain many benefits from doing so.

In the 'developed' world as it is today dawn is, of course, less important to mankind than it used to be. We still need light; but for the most part the light that we need is at our command and instantly available at the touch of a switch. So few of us have the experience of waiting and watching eagerly and anxiously for the dawn. But it is not so very long ago that this experience was widespread and familiar. In the black-out of the last war, when man-made lights 'went out all over Europe', many people spent many hours waiting with eager longing for the dawn – farmers eager to locate their cattle and bring them in for the morning milking; crews of ships and aircraft who had lost their bearings and longed for light enough to detect a landmark; troops in front lines peering anxiously through the darkness for any hint of a night-sortie by the enemy; people of cities upon which bombs were falling in the night yearning for the dawn which would deprive the bombers of the cover of darkness and send them back to where they belonged.

People who so watched for dawn soon came to realise how quietly, unobtrusively and almost imperceptibly it comes. It does not break upon the world suddenly and dramatically, like a clap of thunder or a flash of lightning. Those who long for its coming keep scanning the sky close to the horizon – the eastern sky if they know their bearings, the whole horizon if they do not. They strain their eyes to detect any easement of the surrounding darkness, any hint that it is beginning to lift. But the first hint of its lifting is often misleading. It may be merely a figment of the watcher's over-strained eyes; it may be due simply to a passing break in the cloud-cover or to fires in the distance caused by falling bombs. The watchers must watch a little longer for the spreading and growing of that first faint light on the eastern horizon: only then can they be sure that the dawn has indeed come and say to themselves or their colleagues, with relief and gladness, 'That *was* the dawn that appeared five minutes ago.' One might say that it is only in retrospect, with hindsight, that dawn can be recognised and welcomed for what it is.

In my Christmas sermon I applied these thoughts to our Saviour's birth. It was a very quiet, unobtrusive event; it took place at night and in the humblest of circumstances; there was no light to be seen save perhaps the faint glow of a candle in the stable; and though angels may have sung for joy in heaven there was no public excitement or celebration on earth. It was only later, in retrospect and with hindsight, that the birth in Bethlehem could be recognised and welcomed as the dawn of 'healing for all mankind'; it was only on the first Easter Day that the child of Bethlehem could be recognised as Emmanuel, as 'God with us' and the meaning of the first Christmas Day welcomed by mankind with relief and rejoicing.

Such, then, was the theme of my Christmas Day sermon. But in drawing attention to the phrase 'has dawned' in the sentence from the Epistle to Titus I had ignored the phrase 'The grace of God' with which the sentence begins. I had done so because I had no clear idea of its meaning. Of course I had heard it read, or read it myself, in the Bible times without number: I had used it myself, or heard it used, often enough in ordinary conversation – 'There but for the grace of God go I,' 'By the grace of God we were all awake when the fire broke out,' 'It was only by the grace of God that that fool of a driver didn't run into us.' The phrase is familiar enough, but if someone had asked me what it means I should probably have answered that it is simply an alternative phrase, or an old-fashioned phrase, for 'the goodness of God'. But some weeks after I had preached my Christmas sermon I came to feel that this answer is inadequate – that when St Paul wrote to Titus that 'the grace of God has dawned upon the world with healing for all mankind' he had in mind something more precise than the 'goodness of God'. In my sermon I had, in fact, assumed that he did so; I had assumed that he was referring specifically to the particular event of the birth of our Saviour, that he was saying that the grace of God had dawned upon the world in the stable at Bethlehem. If my assumption was wrong, if St Paul meant no more than that God has shown his goodness to the world, then his words were no more appropriate to Christmas Day than to any other day of the year. If 'the grace of God' is simply 'the goodness of God', then it was known and taught in the religion of the Jews centuries before the first Christmas Day.

So I tried to clarify my idea of the meaning of 'the grace of God' by looking at the passages in the Bible in which the phrase is used. With the help of my old and perhaps out-of-date concordance and its verification by a modern, computer-based concordance, I soon discovered that in the Old Testament there are none: the phrase 'the grace of God' is *never* used. On twenty or so occasions the word 'grace' is used on its own: Joseph, for instance, 'finds grace' in the eyes of Potiphar, and Esther in the eyes of the Persian king. But on all these occasions the word 'grace' refers to the attitude of one person to another, and in recent translations of the Bible it is usually replaced by 'favour'. Never in the Old Testament does the word 'grace' refer, explicitly or by implication, to an attitude or attribute or characteristic of God; the word 'grace' is occasionally used but it is never used of God.

In sharp contrast to this I found that in the New Testament, the length of which is only about a quarter of the length of the Old, the phrase 'the grace of God' is used scores of times, and on scores of other occasions we read of 'grace from God', of 'the grace of our Lord Jesus Christ' and of 'grace which we have received'. In the New Testament 'grace' is a very prominent word and almost always has a deeply *religious* significance: it has become a very important term in the language of theology.

At first I was somewhat surprised by the sharpness of this contrast between the two Testaments of the Bible. But later I realised that it was only to be expected, for I remembered the majestic prologue of St John's gospel. There one reads 'The Word was made flesh and dwelt among us, and we beheld his glory, the glory as of the only begotten of the Father, full of *grace* and truth . . . And of his fullness have we all received, and *grace* upon *grace* . . . For the law was given by Moses but *grace* and truth came by Jesus Christ.' St John makes it quite explicit that the grace of God was unknown to the world until it came into the world in and through Jesus Christ; so it was only to be expected that there would be no reference to the grace of God in the Old Testament. Through the law given by Moses the writers of the Old Testament knew something – many things – about God, but they knew nothing of his grace.

So my idea that 'the grace of God' was simply an alternative or old-fashioned expression for 'the goodness of God' was not only vague: it was also misleading. For the goodness of God was certainly known to the writers of the Old Testament – one need only think of Psalm 107 and its refrain 'O that men would praise the Lord for his goodness and declare the wonders that he doeth for the children of men'. 'The grace of God' *must* mean something distinct from, or more precise than, 'the goodness of God'.

I considered the word 'grace' in itself. It is a very ancient word. Etymologists who study the history of words have traced 'grace' back to Sanscrit, the ancient language of India which is believed to be the root and origin of all except three of the multitude of languages which have since been used in Europe. The root-word in Sanscrit, from which the English word 'grace' – along with similar words in other European languages – has developed, is *gurtas*; and this is a very interesting word. For it embraces in its meaning both something which is *welcome* and the *gladness* with which such a thing is met or received. *Gurtas* would refer, for instance, both to the falling of rain at long last upon a parched land and to the delight with which the people of the land dance in the rain in celebration of its coming; or it would refer both to a song sung by a fine voice and to the pleasure and appreciation of those who hear it. The single word *gurtas* embraces both the welcome thing which happens and the response which it naturally and inevitably evokes.

Such then is the meaning of the ancient word from which

our word 'grace' has sprung along with similar-sounding words in many other European languages. *Gurtas* refers to a situation *as a whole*: a situation in which an event or initiative wins by its own quality a wholly positive and appropriate response: a situation in which *gurtas* both initiates and is met by *gurtas*. One might say that the situation called *gurtas* is a creative, self-sustaining situation. One might liken *gurtas* to the situation or relationship which we call 'friendship': the longer friendship lasts the deeper and stronger it becomes.

Now in the course of history ancient roots have developed in many languages what we might call offshoots. In Latin, for instance, two words have sprung from the root of *gurtas*. One is *gratus*, the other is *gratia*. The first refers to that which initiates *gurtas*, the second to that which responds to *gurtas*. It seems that the Romans saw a distinction within the situation which the ancient Indians saw as a whole: a distinction between that which initiates *gurtas* and that which responds to it. The Romans saw the situation as two-sided and made use of slightly different words when referring to one side or the other; so they used *gratus* of something which is welcome, and *gratia* of the response which it naturally evokes. Admittedly, the distinction is not precise nor always made by Latin writers, but broadly speaking *gratia* refers to one's thanks for a gift or service which has itself been *gratus*.

In modern English several offshoots have grown from the root of *gurtas* and the distinctions between them are quite precise. Our word 'grace' survives, so to speak, in direct line from the ancient root, but round it are clustered a number of offshoots. We have 'graceful' and 'gracefulness', 'gracious' and 'graciousness', 'grateful' and 'gratitude'. 'Graceful' and its noun refer to something that is aesthetically welcome – a graceful dancer or a graceful cover drive on the cricket field.

'Gracious' and its noun refer to something which is morally or emotionally welcome – a friendly letter from someone who might have taken offence or warm hospitality at the house of a stranger. 'Grateful' and 'gratitude', on the other hand, refer to our *response* to what has been welcome. In our language the distinction between the 'two sides' of the situation of *gurtas* is clear and sharp. It is so clear and so sharp that it may obscure the fact that gratitude is the natural response to gracefulness or graciousness: it may give the impression that the response of gratitude which is appropriate to gracefulness or graciousness is a duty rather than a joy, a burden rather than a blessing.

But in the Greek language used by the writers of the New Testament no distinction is made between the 'two sides' of the situation of *gurtas*. The Greek word *'charis'*, like the root-word *gurtas*, embraces in its meaning both sides of the situation – both that which initiates the situation and that which naturally responds thereto. *Charis* means 'gracefulness' and 'graciousness' and 'gratefulness'. *Charis* is used of a dance which is aesthetically welcome, and of a letter which is morally welcome, and of the gratitude which such things naturally evoke. The ordinary phrase for 'thank you' in classical Greek was *charin oida* which literally means 'I am aware of *charis*'. *Charis* is met by *charis*. As I have already said, we very often read in the New Testament of the grace of God – in Greek of the *charis* of God – but we also read of *charis* being offered by the writer *to* God. So, for instance, at the end of the ninth chapter of St Paul's second epistle to the Corinthians he writes of 'God's overflowing *charis* to you' and in the next sentence offers *'charis* to God' for this unspeakable gift. In our English translations of course we read in the first sentence of 'God's overflowing grace' and in the second of 'thanks to God for his unspeakable gift'. In English we use two quite different words to express what is meant in Greek by the one word *charis*.

Let us go just one step further in exploring the meaning of words. In Greek the word *charis* is closely connected with the noun *chara* which means 'joy' and the verb *chairo* which means 'to be glad'. Where *charis* is, there is joy and gladness: the joy which initiates evokes the response of gladness. What we call 'thanks' or 'gratitude' is not so much a duty which is owed as a gladness which is shared. Those to whom the *charis* of God was first disclosed in Jesus Christ found themselves wholly and 'unspeakably' glad.

Now let us go back to the fact that 'the grace of God' was a phrase unknown to the writers of the Old Testament. This does not of course imply that they know nothing about God. Far from it: they knew that God is One and there is no other; that it is by his power and his wisdom that the world was created and sustained; that he had chosen their own nation to be the instrument of his purpose and the particular recipient of his concern and care; and that, unlike the gods of the heathen, he was, in his relationship with themselves, morally *good* – just, merciful, kind, loving. In the Old Testament, especially in the book of the Psalms, there are constant references not only to the power and wisdom of God but also to his moral goodness – to what might be called the virtues of God. What the Old Testament writers knew of God might be summarised in the words repeated several times in Psalm 107: 'O that men would praise the Lord for his goodness and declare the wonders that he doeth for the children of men.'

Virtue – moral goodness in one or other of its manifold forms – deserves and wins respect, admiration, praise. To speak of someone as just or kind or merciful or loving is to praise him or her. In principle we respect virtue: no politician would win votes by announcing that he or she was 'against justice' or 'merciless' or 'unkind' or 'opposed to love'. But what we respect in principle is not always welcome when we encounter it in practice. What we respect from a distance, so to speak, is not always welcome when we meet it face to face. What we respect in theory is not always welcome existentially.

Let us consider this divergence between our theoretical respect for virtue and our existential response to it. Like everybody else I respect goodness in general, but many a time I have found an expression of goodness by no means welcome but, on the contrary, embarrassing and even repulsive. I remember once receiving from an old lady a modest gift for the church. Having put it into my hands she then listed what she had 'gone without' to accumulate her gift. It was very embarrassing. I felt that by thus parading her goodness she was polluting it, and on the other hand I also felt that by having this suspicion I was being unjust and ungrateful – perhaps she was just chattering on as old ladies often do. I remember more than one 'prayer meeting' at which the people and causes for which we were asked to pray were so recherché that it seemed to me that we were competing in displaying the range of our compassion; yet perhaps I was quite wrong and the compassion of every speaker was heartfelt and genuine. Perhaps it was my fault that, on these occasions as with the old lady, I suspected that goodness was not expressing itself but rather advertising and thus degrading itself. But, like everyone else, I am as I am, and I cannot in practice welcome goodness if and when it draws attention to itself, flaunts, parades and advertises itself.

Let us consider the form of goodness which we call justice. We all respect justice – in international law, in the administration of the law of the land, in conformity to the laws of a competitive game or sport, in business transactions, in the disciplines of school and home and so on. To call a person or an institution 'just' or 'fair' is to praise him or her for it. Now Aristotle defined justice as 'a kind of equality', but we find in practice, in close encounters with justice, that the 'kind of equality' is that which applied in Animal Farm – 'all are equal but some are more equal than others'. In encounters with justice we are all prejudiced in our own favour. When in a court of law the jury retires to consider its verdict the prisoner in the dock, and the prisoner's family and friends, go through a period of intense and almost unbearable anxiety. They wait for the verdict as if nothing in the world matters except that verdict: and when it is given there is an explosion of relief or despair which cannot be concealed. The judge may ponder in his own mind whether the verdict was justified – whether justice was done or not done – but to the prisoner and those around him or her that question is irrelevant. What matters to them existentially, what is revealed in their faces and 'body language', is whether the prisoner was found guilty or not guilty. Though in principle we all respect justice and deplore injustice, there are occasions when, in practice, affection for a son or loyalty to a friend may motivate us so powerfully that we rejoice in an acquittal which was in fact unjust or fall into angry despair at a verdict which was just.

The virtue of mercy or forgiveness is often attributed to God in the Old Testament. Again we respect this virtue in principle. At the present time both of the words 'mercy' and 'forgiveness' have come to have a significance which is almost political. We have become aware of civil wars in which no mercy is shown to captives or helpless refugees or little children and of bitter animosities within nations which have their roots in unforgiven wrongs of long ago. What happens where there is no mercy and what is likely to happen where there is no forgiveness is made painfully evident on our televisions, and many governments are under the pressure of public opinion to find some way of introducing mercy into a situation where there is none and encouraging mutual forgiveness in a land in which it is slow to appear. One might almost say that, in principle, the world as a whole has never been more respectful of the virtues of mercy and forgiveness.

Yet in practice the expression of these virtues is not always welcome or easy to receive. It may be, or be taken to be, an act of condescension – an expression of the superior power of the person who shows mercy over the one to whom mercy is shown, an assertion by the person who forgives that he or she is in the right and the person who is forgiven in the wrong. An expression of mercy or forgiveness may be, or be taken to be, a veiled insult to the person to whom it is made – a humiliation which is painful to receive. Works of mercy and words of forgiveness may also impose upon the recipient a burden of obligation and indebtedness – a continuing anxiety lest he or she may never be able to pay back or 'make up for' that which has been received. Charles Dickens created in his novel *Martin Chuzzlewit* the smooth and slimy character of Mr Pecksniff who, having exploited a man, responds to his victim's protests by forgiving him for making them. Eventually the victim shouts 'I *will not* be forgiven,' turns on his heels and goes away. In Dostoevsky's great novel *The Idiot* the hero, Myshkin, is grossly libelled in an article to which five men have contributed. These men thrust themselves upon him, and there follows a remarkable dialogue in which Myshkin's gentle correction of the errors in the libel is taken by the men as a gratuitous affront and insult to themselves. Myshkin bears no malice against those who have libelled him: he is a genuinely and consistently forgiving man. Yet in the dialogue he becomes increasingly aware of his clumsiness in expressing what he means, of his failure to communicate with these particular men. The long dialogue ends not in reconciliation but in the *status quo*. It would be naive to suppose that the virtues of mercy and forgiveness, when expressed and encountered in particular situations, are always welcome and responded to with gratitude.

Of all the virtues, kindness is probably the most frequently mentioned and praised. Yet one remembers the old joke 'X is always doing kindnesses to people: you can tell them by their hunted look.' At a serious level we must recognise that acts of kindness are not always welcome to those to whom they are shown: they can be, or seem to be, threatening, restrictive, managerial. This is particularly the case for people who are ill, infirm or in some way handicapped or incapacitated. People in such a situation naturally evoke kindness, and for the most part they receive it gladly and gratefully. But it is well known to people who have no sight that they are sometimes treated as if they had no brain either; to people who lose an arm or leg that they are sometimes treated as if they could never again take part in any sport; to people of a certain age that they are sometimes treated as if they were no longer competent to make significant decisions for themselves. Such treatment, however kindly meant, is by no means welcome or received with gratitude. It threatens the independence of the recipient: it limits, or threatens to limit, his or her freedom. There are some partnerships in which one who is infirm is so wholly taken over and managed by the kindness of the other that he or she becomes entirely passive and will speak to a visitor only when the active partner is out of the room. The recipient of kindness is sometimes, as the phrase goes, 'killed with kindness'.

Finally, let us consider the virtue of love. A loving relationship between people is universally admired: it wins not only respect but also a certain awe and wonder. Where love is mutual it transcends all other virtues and creates the most welcome of all human relationships. But love is not always mutual: love is not always met by answering love. When love is not met by answering love, it is painful to the lover, and to the beloved it is at best embarrassing and at worst threatening. Love is a dangerous virtue and the expression of it can be tragic and even destructive both to the lover and to the beloved. The expression of love is welcome only when it meets with answering love. In theory we all want to be loved, but we find existentially that an expression of love, however authentic, may be unwelcome, embarrassing or threatening. So it is that many a person looks for another place of work because so-and-so is 'making eyes at me' or 'after me' or 'chasing me' or whatever is the contemporary phrase; so it is that many a teenager leaves home because 'my dad is always asking me where I have been' or 'my mum is always fussing about my clothes'.

The point I am trying to make is that virtues we respect and admire in principle are not always welcome or attractive when we encounter the expression of them in practice, in particular situations. It may be that this is our own fault. It may be that it is the effect of our 'fallen' human nature that we find goodness unattractive when it advertises itself, or justice abhorrent when it condemns a friend, or forgiveness unacceptable when it humiliates us. But whatever the reason, the fact remains. We are as we are. In particular situations, in close encounters, our principles become fragile, feeble, weak.

So it comes about that those divine virtues of which the Old Testament writers were well aware are respected but not necessarily attractive. No one would deny that they are worthy of respect, yet in close encounters with them we often feel ourselves embarrassed or humiliated or insulted or threatened. We may deserve to undergo such feelings of unease and anxiety, but they are not welcome nor do they naturally evoke our gratitude. One might say that the writers of the Old Testament knew of the power and virtues of God but not of his grace. They did not know that in his dealings with mankind he initiates that situation which is called *gurtas* in Sanscrit and *charis* in Greek: the situation which is attractive and welcome to mankind and naturally evokes in us gratitude and joy.

So the grace of God which became known through Jesus Christ is not to be thought of as simply another power to be added to the list of divine powers and virtues which are already known. It is to be thought of as the *manner* in which all those powers and virtues are expressed. They are expressed in such a manner or in such a way that they are attractive and welcome to those who know of them and naturally evoke gratitude and joy: the *charis* of God is such that it wins the response of *charis* from mankind: that is to say, in our English language, the grace of God wins from mankind the response of gratitude and joy. To know the grace of God is in itself to be filled with joyful gratitude.

Now can we find any general terms in which to describe this manner which naturally evokes gratitude and joy in others? It is not easy to do so, but sometimes one meets people who are profoundly grateful for certain episodes in their lives and very glad to tell one about them. As they look back they remember certain people who helped them in those episodes and for whom they are full of praise. A friend of mine, a fine man, now dead, knew nothing of his parents and had been brought up in an orphanage; and, rather to my surprise, he spoke very highly of the staff of the orphanage. He used of the staff phrases such as, 'they knew what lads are like', 'they tried to see things from our point of view', 'they made you feel they were on your side', 'we got on well with them'. I had many conversations with this friend and he told me of many particular incidents which I have now forgotten, but my general impression of him is that, though an orphan, he was brought up with understanding and consideration, with a certain grace for which he could not help being grateful.

I remember a more recent conversation with a relative stranger – a woman whose husband had died of cancer in a hospice. She had looked after him for a long time at home and would not agree at first to the suggestion that he should go into a hospice: as she said, she had no idea what hospices were like. But when in the end she agreed and visited her husband in the hospice she was almost overwhelmed by the quality of the hospice care: everyone was so considerate, so attentive to his funny little likes and dislikes, so tactful in what they said to him, so understanding, so thoughtful. They could not have looked after him better if he had been their own father. There was a certain grace in the care of the hospice and, when the old man died, his widow was profoundly grateful and eager to tell people not so much about her own loss as about the wonder of the hospice care.

Two people, my friend and the widow, responded to grace

with gratitude and gladness. They described the grace which they had met in such terms as 'knowing what lads are like', 'seeing things from our point of view', 'being considerate', 'being on our side', 'being tactful', 'being understanding', and so on. These are homely words and phrases, commonly used to indicate what it is in someone's manner of behaving that makes it welcome to us and wins our gratitude. They are familiar in ordinary conversation. But in the language of theology they seem out of place: it would be unusual to hear from a theologian that God sees things from our point of view or that he is very considerate or very tactful. Theologians very often refer to the grace of God, but rarely if ever do they illustrate the meaning of the phrase in such homely terms as I have used. Nor do they illustrate that meaning in terms of their own. In the past, in the centuries when theology was the principal subject of intellectual debate, they distinguished between various forms and effects of the grace of God – between 'sanctifying grace' and 'actual grace' and 'prevenient grace' and so on – and these distinctions were the subject of endless controversy, but they seem to have thought of the grace of God itself as a kind of mysterious *substance* which God imparts to certain people by certain means and which saves those people from damnation. They seem to have lost touch altogether with the meaning of the word *charis* to the New Testament writers when they used it so often and so gladly.

Now those writers themselves were also silent about the meaning of the word *charis* when it is used of God. They did not analyse its meaning or illustrate and clarify what it means in such homely terms as I have suggested or in more dignified statements of their own. They had no reason to do so, for they could actually point to the *charis* of God. In

Jesus Christ they had seen it for themselves, experienced it for themselves. St John wrote in the opening words of his first epistle, 'that which we have heard, that which we have seen with our eyes and our hands have handled . . . that is what we declare to you', and, as we have noticed before, he wrote in the opening words of his gospel that Jesus Christ had dwelt among us full of the *charis* of God, that the *charis* of God had come by Jesus Christ and that of his fullness we have all received *charis* meeting *charis*

So St John and his colleagues did not need to explain or clarify in their own words what 'the grace of God' meant: it simply meant that new thing, that new truth, which is shown in and received from Jesus Christ. Their purpose was to make Jesus Christ known to people who, unlike themselves, had not seen or heard about him; and their method was not to make general statements about his character, his upbringing, his way with people and so on. Their method was to tell the *story*, so far as they were able, of what happened, of what he said and did and what was done to him, in the years when he dwelt among us. We shall see in the next chapter that it is very important that the first Christian preachers and teachers used this method of making Jesus Christ known and thereby enabling us to enter into the full meaning of the words of St Paul, 'The grace of God has dawned upon the world with healing for all mankind'.

Chapter Two

THE POWER OF STORIES

❧

IT IS OFTEN SAID, rightly, that Christianity is a historical religion. This does not mean, of course, that it has been in existence for a long time and by its long survival proves its worth; nor does it mean that, since Christianity came into being long ago, it must now be out of date. It means that the distinctive truth which the Christian religion believes and teaches can only be expressed and conveyed in the form of a story. The words 'history' and 'story' spring from the same ancient root and have the same original meaning: but they came into the English language by two different routes – 'history' by way of the Latin language and 'story' by way of the Celtic. Since 'story' was the first to arrive in the English language it is the word which I shall use.

A great deal of ordinary conversation consists of the telling, hearing and exchanging of stories. Stories report events – *particular* things which have happened in this eventful world. In contrast, statements convey *general* truths about the world itself and every thing or person that the world contains. So, for instance, 'there was a major earthquake in Japan last night' is a story whereas 'Japan is very often affected by earthquakes' is a statement. 'Johnnie scored three goals this afternoon' is a story whereas 'Johnnie is a very good footballer' is a statement. Both stories and statements contain and convey information but, as we shall see, the effect of information conveyed by a story tends to be rather more powerful than that of information conveyed by a statement.

Consider so simple an example as this. A little girl comes home from school weeping, runs up to her bedroom and will not come down for tea. Clearly something is wrong. Her parents ask, 'What's the matter, love?', and eventually they get the answer, 'Our teacher is not fair.' That statement gives the parents *some* information: they know now that 'the matter' is not toothache or a quarrel with a friend on the way home. But they need to know more, and almost inevitably the next question will be, 'What happened, love? Tell us what happened.' And then the child will tell the story, and it is in response to the story they hear that the parents will either, at one extreme, write a letter to the head demanding the teacher's instant dismissal or, at the other, give the little girl a smile and a hug and promise her ice cream for tea. The child's statement that her teacher was unfair was not untrue or misleading, but her parents needed to know the degree, the *particularity*, of her 'unfairness' before they could make the appropriate response, and it was only the story that could inform them of that.

Consider another example. It is made known in an office that a new manager called Ebenezer Smith will shortly be taking over. One of the staff, Tom Brown, recognises from the unusual name that this is the man who was manager at the place where he previously worked and he mentions this to his colleagues. Almost inevitably someone will ask Tom what this new man is like. Tom will be rather careful in answering. He wants to be fair to Smith, and he does not want to mislead his colleagues – for if he does so, he himself will seem a fool when Smith arrives. So he chooses his words with some hesitation: 'Well, he's a quiet chap ... doesn't throw his weight about ... I wouldn't call him unfriendly but he's a bit ... reserved ... as I say, he's quiet, but he's got ... quite a strong side to him too.' And then, as likely as not, Brown will add more confidently, 'I'll tell you what he did at the other place one afternoon when two hefty drunks came blundering into the office.' And then Tom will tell a story, confident that it will convey a more vivid and exact impression of Smith than the combination of general statements which he has already made. It is not *mis*information that those statements conveyed but it was, in his opinion, less exact and adequate information than was conveyed by the story.

Stories of particular events tend to be more powerful in evoking a response than do statements in general terms. Appeals on the media for famine relief and similar causes tend to be most effective when they are focused on the suffering of a particular family or a particular child: the statement that a million people are starving evokes a less swift and generous response than the story in pictures or words of what a particular family is going through. The statement itself is not misleading; but the power of its meaning is stronger when it is illustrated or reinforced by the story.

Every story that is worth telling has a meaning. It is not a mere jumble of words. A story in English is not worth telling to someone who knows no English: it would mean nothing to him or her. A story is only worth telling if it means something to the hearer. Now sometimes the hearer is uncertain about what the story means – perhaps it contains technical terms – and asks 'What does that mean?' The natural reply is, 'It means that ...' The teller of the story clarifies the meaning of the story with a statement. Many a person, having been to hospital for an examination, tells someone else that the complaint was diagnosed as such and such, its cause attributed to such and such and the therapy advised was such and such, and many a time the response to the story is, 'What does this mean? Will you have to be off work? Will you have to go into hospital?' and so on. The meaning of a story can be *clarified* by statements but it cannot be *distilled* into statements or adequately *conveyed* by statements. The meaning of a story can only be received from the story itself; it can only be fully conveyed by attention to the story itself.

I find this fact very important. It came to me many years ago, but it came in so moving a way that I still remember it vividly. I think it is worth telling this story which illustrates so powerfully the power of stories. I knew in the evening of their days two brothers, Walter and Robert, who were the only children of parents who were not so much neglectful as cruel. The suffering which the two shared in childhood had created between them a bond which endured long after they were married and had children of their own. They worked for years and years in the same mill, never lived more than a few hundred yards from each other and, when I knew them in their retirement, spent countless hours going fishing together in the local mill ponds and canals.

One Saturday when they were fishing together some kind of quarrel or 'difference' broke out between them and had not been resolved by the time when they parted company close to their homes. On the same night the elder brother, Walter, had some kind of internal haemorrhage. His wife called the doctor who gave some immediate medication and sent for the ambulance, but though the ambulance arrived within minutes Walter had died by the time it reached the hospital.

When Robert was told in the morning his reaction was almost hysterical. He was overwhelmed by shock and grief and particularly by guilt, for he was convinced that it was he who had caused the quarrel, that it was the quarrel that had caused the haemorrhage and the haemorrhage that had caused Walter's death. He was adamant that he was a murderer, and as the day went on and he brooded on his guilt he became more and more distressed. When I called in the evening and his wife made some reference to Walter's funeral Robert flared up in anger: he did not want to hear about the funeral; he would not be going to it; his brother's murderer had no right to go; he had no right now to call Walter his brother; he had put an end to all that by killing him.

Of course I joined the family in trying to comfort him. We could not deny that Robert might have started the quarrel – none of us had been there. Nor could we deny realistically that the distress of the quarrel *might* have hastened Walter's death. What we could and did say, truthfully, was that Walter was a very understanding man, very kind-hearted and for-giving, and that the last thing he would have wished was that Robert should feel as he did. But this brought no comfort to Robert – rather the reverse: he agreed that Walter was 'a right good man', but that made his sense of guilt for having killed him more intense. At the end of the day the doctor had to be called to give him medication.

I called again next evening. His wife told me that Robert had sat all day in his chair brooding, morose and silent, blazing with anger when one of the family asked him some-thing about Walter's funeral. We sat around for a while scarcely daring to speak lest Robert should flare up again. But then there was a tap on the door and Walter's widow came in. She was a good deal younger than Walter – a bright, brisk, very practical woman. She had in her hand what was obviously a fishing rod in a green case. She went straight to Robert, held out the case and said, 'Here, Robert, this is for you.' Robert looked, stood up from his chair, backed away and said, 'No . . . I know what this is . . . it was his . . . no . . . I am the last man that should have it.' But Alice said briskly and firmly, 'Now, Robert, listen to me. I am going to tell you what happened on Saturday night.' She told him the story. I cannot vouch for her exact words, but they went something like this: 'After the doctor had done what he could and we were waiting for the ambulance there were a few minutes when your Walter seemed a bit easier, and he said to me, "Alice, will you fetch me that rod of mine that's in a green case." Well, I thought he was wandering in his mind but to humour him I fetched it and asked him if this was the right one. He looked at it and said, "Yes, this is the one: it's my favourite rod. Now, Alice, I want you to take it round to our Robert, and tell him that I want him to have it and make sure that he takes it." So he's given it to you, Robert, and you've *got* to take it.' Robert slowly came forward – his head down like that of a shamed child. He took the rod and quickly went out of the room.

I saw no more of Robert that night, but afterwards he was all right. He would talk naturally about Walter as 'my brother' or 'our Walter'; he discussed the funeral with Walter's widow and attended it with quiet dignity and, when some weeks later I met him on his way to go fishing on his own, he stopped to show me 'that rod of our Walter's that he gave me'. Of course he was still left sad and lonely by his brother's death, and it was not very long before he himself died. But he lived his last few months free from the terrible burden of guilt which had at first lain upon him.

It is clear that the story which Alice told that night meant a great deal to Robert. It had a very powerful effect on him: it freed him from his sense of guilt and saved him from despair. He already knew that his brother was a very understanding, kind-hearted and forgiving man; but these statements, true though they were, did nothing to alleviate his distress. When Robert's family made these statements they were powerless to ease his burden of guilt – in fact they made that burden even heavier. It was only when Robert heard from Alice the story of the particular things that Walter had said and done before he died that the burden of guilt was lifted from him. The meaning of the story to Robert *could* not be distilled into and conveyed to him by general statements about Walter: it could be conveyed only by the telling and hearing of the story itself.

Through this moving experience I came to see how important it can be to attend to stories themselves rather than to distillations, summaries or similar statements of what they mean. In this respect stories are akin to poems. Any poem that is worth publishing means something: it is not a mere jumble or jangle of words. And the task of tutors in English studies is to help students to discover, receive and understand the meaning of certain poems. They do so in various ways: perhaps by reading the poem aloud or asking the students to do so; by speaking of the life and circumstances of the poet and the situation in which he or she wrote the poem; by clarifying the meaning of technical terms or archaic expressions within the poem; by drawing attention to contrasts, echoes and evocations among the images which the poet presents. But no tutor would say to the students, 'This poem is in the syllabus. But the poem is long and time is short, so instead of reading the poem you had better take down my summary of what it means.' No tutor would be so arrogant as to presume that his or her words can convey the meaning of the poem better than those which the poet has actually written. There was an occasion when T. S. Eliot was accosted at a reception by a lady who claimed to be a great admirer of his work. 'But,' she said, 'I have one question to ask you: and I do hope you can give me a straight answer. In your poem *Ash Wednesday* you wrote this: "Lady, three white leopards sat under a juniper tree in the cool of the day." Now what did you mean by that?' Eliot furrowed his brow as if he were pondering: then he said gravely, 'Yes, Madam, I can give you a straight answer. I meant "Lady, three white leopards sat under a juniper tree in the cool of the day:" and if I had meant something else I should have written something else.'

Poems say what they mean and mean what they say; so also do stories. Their meaning cannot be summarised in general statements and conveyed intact in a different verbal container. The story itself must be told or written and heard or read: only so can its meaning be fully received and understood. But its meaning is not, so to speak, written in stone: the impact and effect of the story will be different at different times and for different people. The story which Alice told was heard by several of us, but it meant much more to Robert than to myself and, I imagine, the rest of us. The meaning of the story of the Holocaust is so terrible that some people have tried to shield themselves from the power of its impact by claiming that the story itself is not true. The story of a rock-climber's achievement or calamity will have for other rock-climbers a different meaning from that which it has for the general public.

So to understand a story is not to know a statement or formula which expresses the meaning of the story. It is to be attentive to the story and open to receive its impact and its meaning. The word 'understand' – that is 'stand under' – is suggestive of a certain *posture*. It is not the posture of probing into or analysing; nor is it the posture of grasping, comprehending and mastering. When we speak of someone as 'an understanding friend' or as 'very understanding' we do not mean that that person probes into us and identifies 'what makes us tick': nor do we mean that he or she has mastery and control over us. We mean that our understanding friend is attentive to us and open to receive whatever it may be that we wish to tell or disclose or share. He or she has time enough and respect enough to wait upon us and receive and respond to whatever we may wish to say at that particular time.

So to understand a story is to allow it to make its own impact upon us, to receive from it whatever it may 'say' to us at a particular time or in a particular situation. I have mentioned already that tutors in English can help their students to understand the meaning of a particular poem. They do not tell them what the poem means, but they do enable or encourage them to understand its meaning. They enable them to feel that the poem is *worth* attending to and so to expose themselves to the impact and power of its meaning. What the poem means or 'says' to each student will be slightly different, and for each its meaning will be slightly different at different times of life. But as long as the poem is remembered or returned to, it – as long as it is understood – will continue to 'say' something to those who were introduced to it as students. Similarly, someone who knows a story well may help the hearers to understand its meaning. The very tone and manner in which the story is told may enable the hearers to feel that it is *worth* attending to; their attention may be drawn to details and contrasts within the story; the meaning of particular words and phrases may be clarified; *mis*understandings may be corrected; hearers may be helped to expose themselves to the impact and power of what the story means, of what it 'says' to each hearer in his or her particular circumstances and at different stages of his or her life. So long as the story is remembered and understood it will continue to 'say' something to those who first heard it long ago.

At the beginning of this chapter I made the point that Christianity is a historical religion: that is to say that the distinctive truth which it has to tell can only be told, conveyed and communicated intact in the form of a particular story. It cannot be distilled into, and communicated in, general statements. In the early years of this century many English theologians, under the influence of the German philosopher Hegel, were inclined to disparage particular events and the stories of them and to define all the truth which matters in highly general and comprehensive terms and statements. Some theologians, though Christians by profession, were critical of what they called 'The Scandal of Particularity' which they encountered in Christianity. They considered that orthodox Christianity made too much of particular events associated with Jesus Christ. True religion, in their view, consisted in the recognition of the preeminence of spirit over matter, of the community over the individual, of self-sacrifice over self-fulfilment. So in the writings and teaching of these theologians Jesus Christ was presented as simply one instance among others of the nobility of self-sacrifice: what he did and what he taught was a fine illustration of the pre-eminence of self-sacrifice over self-fulfilment – *so* fine that those who had known him best were moved to share their knowledge of him with others and, eventually, to spread that knowledge throughout the world.

Now this 'Hegelian' theology lingered on in academic circles right through the first half of this century, and when I first dipped my feet into theology it was into this kind of theology that they were dipped. The emphasis was on the moral teaching of Jesus Christ and upon its social and political implications in the world of today: could a Christian be a Communist? Should a Christian be a Pacifist? What should be the relationships between Christians and people of other faiths? And so on. It was almost taken for granted that it was by the moral teaching of Jesus Christ that the early Christians were converted and won to their allegiance to him, and some theologians were even inclined to suggest that, apart from the moral teaching, all that we read about Jesus Christ in the New Testament is so overlain with 'folk-tales' and 'myths' that it is unworthy of serious consideration.

But I was fortunate enough in the course of my theological training to come under the influence of C. H. Dodd and to spend a lot of time sitting at his feet. I still remember him vividly and with deep gratitude. He was small in stature, brisk and cheerful in manner, meticulous in his studies and precise and clear in the conclusions which he drew from them. His knowledge of the Bible, and of the New Testament in particular, was unsurpassed in his day. To his students and the readers of his books he demonstrated beyond all doubt that it was not the moral teaching of Jesus that the first Christian preachers offered and presented to their hearers: it was not by that moral teaching that people were converted and their allegiance won. It was the *story* of particuar events involving Jesus that the first preachers told, and it was by that story that people were converted. It was only to people who had already responded positively and appropriately to the story that – often at those people's own request – the preachers presented the moral teaching of Jesus.

Dodd helped his students to envisage the manner and circumstances in which those preachers told the story – the good news – of Jesus. Within the Roman Empire in which both preachers and hearers lived there were no national frontiers nor legal restrictions nor linguistic barriers to limit the freedom of would-be travellers: people could go wherever their feet or a horse or a ship would carry them. Travel was possible for all but, as the word 'travel' implies, it was hard work for all and exposed the traveller to many dangers. It must have been with a good deal of relief that two or three preachers arrived at last at the town which was their destination or indeed at any town where they might find rest and refreshment *en route*.

In the warm and sunny climate of lands round the Mediterranean Sea every town worthy of the name had its focal point – its so-called market-place. The market-place was much more than an area of alfresco buying and selling: it was the place where, day by day, deals were made and money changed and lawyers met their clients and children played their games and politicians debated or quarrelled and philosophers aired their theories and men were shaved by barbers and, above all else, all and sundry exchanged their news. In such a place the arrival of two or three strangers would not go unnoticed – especially if, footsore and weary, they looked as if they had come from a distance. And it would not be long before one or two people drifted over and asked where they had come from. One can easily imagine the kind of conversation that would naturally follow. 'These last three days we've been on our way from Derbe,' says one of the preachers, and another adds, 'But we started off months ago – a long way from here – in the land of the Jews – in Jerusalem. Have you heard of it?' One of the listeners has heard – in fact he knows someone who has actually *been* there. He calls to his friend, 'Come and meet these strangers: they come from Jerusalem.' So the man comes eagerly across the market-place and perhaps his eagerness attracts a few others to come too. A little crowd begins to gather round the preachers, and inevitably someone puts the question, 'What's going on nowadays in Jerusalem? Have you any news?' One of the preachers answers, 'Yes, we have indeed; and it's good news', and perhaps the tone of his voice and the sparkle in his eyes suggest that what he has to say will be interesting and draw more people still to come round and listen.

Then the preacher tells his story. Its essentials are that recently in the land of the Jews a certain Jesus went about doing good and healing all manner of sickness and suffering; that the authorities for some reason turned against him, brought capital charges against him before the Roman governor and demanded the sentence of crucifixion; that he died by crucifixion and his body was given burial; that three days later he was raised from death and came again to certain of his friends and was seen by them and talked with them. And at the end of the story the preacher appeals to his audience to respond to it with 'repentance'.

Such was the essential content of the story which the first Christian teachers told. Dodd called it their *kerugma* or 'public proclamation'. Of course it did not win instant acceptance or even consideration by all who heard it. Some no doubt dismissed the story as incredible and walked away without more ado: some argued among themselves about its credibility, causing a minor disturbance in the market-place for which the preachers themselves were held responsible by the authorities and were taken into custody and sometimes flogged. Some hearers of the story were, no doubt, so credulous as to believe anything and there and then spread the preacher's news around the market-place in a somewhat garbled form; and certainly some hearers asked the preachers to tell them more and in some cases offered them hospitality in their own homes.

As we have seen, the preachers ended their story with an appeal to their hearers for repentance. But the word is not a satisfactory translation of the original Greek word which is *metanoia*. 'Repentance' implies an awareness of being guilty, being ashamed of oneself and resolving to mend one's ways; but *metanoia* is much broader in its meaning. It means any kind of 'change of mind'; it includes in its meaning 'having second thoughts' on any matter at all and 'seeing in a different light' any kind of situation. If someone who had planned to go to the bank next Monday was reminded that next Monday was a bank holiday and accordingly changed his or her plans, this would be an instance of *metanoia* – of 'seeing the situation in a different light'. But it would be misleading to say that the person 'repented' of his or her original plan. So we must not suppose that the preachers' appeal to their hearers for *metanoia* implied that they should be ashamed of their past and resolved to mend their ways: it was rather an invitation to them to bear in mind the story they had heard and see their own situation in the light of what they had heard. So those hearers who wanted to be told more were responding to the preachers' appeal just as the preachers themselves would have wished.

Strictly speaking, we should refer to the preachers as 'evangelists' and their preaching as 'evangelising': for in the Greek language there is a word which refers specifically to 'a messenger who brings good news', and it is this word which is used in the New Testament of the first travelling preachers. They came to the market-places of the world as messengers bringing good news, welcome news which people would be glad to hear; and they presented this news without conditions or demands to all and sundry who would listen. The messenger of whom we know most was, of course, St Paul. He who in his earlier years in and around Jerusalem had tried earnestly to suppress the news became after his conversion its most ardent messenger and most eager to carry the news to – literally – the ends of the earth; and, as he wrote in one of his letters, he believed himself called 'not to baptise but to evangelise'. In another letter he wrote that it was his ambition to evangelise not in towns where the story of Jesus Christ had already been heard but in towns where it had not. It was also his ambition to live independent of the people whom he evangelised – not to burden them with his 'expenses' but to support himself by the work of his own hands. The good news which he brought was God's free gift, and he himself must not exploit it for his own benefit.

But even St Paul, eager though he was to spread the good news yet more widely in the world, did not limit his stay in each town to a few hours. Those who listened in the market-place heard only the essentials of the good news, the salient events in the story of 'the things concerning Jesus', and people who took the story seriously and thoughtfuly wished 'to hear more'. We must remember that, at the time when the earliest evangelists were at work, the gospels which we know had not yet been written; so the story could only be filled out by word of mouth. St Paul played his part in telling more to people who wished to hear more. We know, for instance, that he told people in Corinth what Jesus had said and done at the Last Supper and that he told people in Ephesus a saying of Jesus which never found a place in the gospels which we know – namely, 'It is more blessed to give than to receive'. Though St Paul had never met Jesus 'in the flesh', he had, after his conversion, 'received' many things from those who had known him well: and these things he passed on to people who, having listened in the market, wished to hear more.

And there is another reason why St Paul, having been the messenger of the good news in certain towns, stayed in the town for weeks or months and, in the important city of Ephesus, for as much as two years. There were people who, having heard the good news and taken it seriously, were willing and eager to commit themselves to it and make of the things concerning Jesus the light of their lives: they wished, in the phrase then used, to become 'followers of the Way'. Whether they were few or many, it was natural that these converts should all turn to the messenger to whom they had listened in the market-place for guidance about 'the Way' and how, in practical terms, it was to be followed. Converts tend to become enthusiasts, and a community of enthusiasts is rarely of one mind: so evangelists found it necessary to take on the additional role of what we should call 'pastors'. It fell to them to keep their converts – their 'flocks' – together, bonded to one another by their common commitment to the good news of Jesus Christ.

———

So even St Paul, who saw himself primarily as an evangelist, found himself taking on a pastoral role too: 'Paul the
Preacher' became 'Paul the Pastor'. He exercised his pastorate
not only while he stayed in the town to which he had brought
the good news but also, in many cases, for years after he had
moved on elsewhere. He had kept in touch with his converts
and they with him – by word of mouth passed between
him and them by other travellers and, of course, by his letters
which have survived to be our treasures today. All of them,
with the possible exception of his letter to the Romans, are
pastoral letters – full of personal affection and concern – and
they throw a great deal of light on the Christian religion as
it was in its earliest days.

Scholarly theologians have, of course, given a vast amount
of attention to the letters of St Paul. I can only write of the
impressions which they have long made, and continue to
make, on myself. The first impression is that they are, in
modern parlance, 'full of passion' – intense, urgent, pouring
out from a mind which is full to overflowing, darting from
point to point and image to image at a pace which must at
times have sorely tried the person to whom St Paul was
dictating. His concern over problems among his converts,
and divisions between them – what he calls 'his care for all
the churches' – weighed heavily upon him; his responsibilities
as a pastor evoked from him an urgent and sometimes almost
explosive response. His letters are existential rather than
doctrinaire both in tone and content.

My second impression is that St Paul was deeply concerned
not only for those who had been converted to Christianity
but also for the people among whom those converts lived.
He was well aware that conversion involved *metanoia* – a
response to the good news which changed one's whole

outlook on life. To accept or make this change was in itself a stumbling-block to be overcome and St Paul was deeply concerned lest converts who had overcome it should put other stumbling-blocks in the path of those who had not. Converts tend to be not only enthusiasts but also extremists, and some extremists of St Paul's time were advocating, or implying by their example, that to follow the Way required one to abstain from sexual intercourse, or to divorce a partner who did not follow the Way, or to reject food sold in the market-place for fear lest it may already have been offered in idol worship, or to give up one's work on the ground that the return of the Lord and the end of the world was imminent, or to cut oneself off socially from those who do not follow the Way. St Paul did not question the freedom of extremists to *be* extremists – in a sense he was an extremist himself – but he warned them against becoming stumbling blocks to those whom he called, tactfully, 'the weak'. He warned his converts in general against forms of behaviour which, in the society of his day, would be seen as eccentricities: hence his recommendations that, when his converts gathered together for prayer, men should come with uncovered head and short hair, women with covered head and in total silence. It was a matter of urgent concern to St Paul that the joy of the good news should be available to all mankind, unimpaired by requirements that those who received it should commit themselves to abnormal behaviour and associate themselves with social eccentricities.

My third impression of St Paul and his letters is that, even when he had become a pastor, the story of Jesus rather than the moral teaching of Jesus remained the focus and reference point of his attention and his thinking. In his letters he wrestles with, and gives guidance upon, many matters of morality which have arisen among his converts but only twice, and that briefly, does he mention explicitly that his guidance comes 'from the Lord'. It is likely enough that he *did not know* all those words and precepts of Jesus of which we read in the Sermon on the Mount and the parables and other passages in the gospels: after all, he had no first-hand memories of Jesus in his days in Galilee, and what he received of the story of Jesus from others who had such memories was not necessarily so comprehensive as what was later collected and recorded in the gospels which we read today. St Paul's pastoral guidance to his converts over matters of morality emerged, so to speak, from within himself: it is a combination of practical common sense with the authority of the Spirit of the risen Christ 'dwelling within him'.

It was the story of 'the things concerning Jesus Christ', the essentials of the story preached in the market-place – the good news of which St Paul had been the messenger – that gave to him both the responsibility and the authority for guiding his converts on moral issues. The story of Jesus rejected, crucified and raised from death was never far from the centre of his teeming mind. To change the metaphor, it was the backcloth against which he did all his urgent thinking and his passionate writing. There was an occasion when he was appealing to converts in several towns for financial support on behalf of the poverty-stricken Christians in Jerusalem. The Christians in Corinth had promised support but so far had done nothing to fulfil their promise; so St Paul renewed his appeal to them, and reinforced it by arguments that might well be used by fund-raisers today. He mentioned that the Christians of Macedonia had been *exceedingly* generous; he pointed out that some time the Corinthians themselves might be in need of support from others; he reminded them discreetly that failure to keep their promise would not enhance their good name. But in the middle of these rather mundane arguments there suddenly erupts the sentence. 'You know the grace of our Lord Jesus Christ – that though he was rich yet for your sake he became poor, so that, by his poverty, you might become rich.' On another occasion St Paul was shocked to hear that these same Corinthians had among them a man who was exercising his Christian freedom by 'living with his father's wife', and, what is more, that his fellow converts were rather proud at having among them so bold and brazen a colleague. St Paul responded to the news in as solemn and authoritative a sentence as ever he wrote, demanding that this man should immediately be excluded from the Christian community: he was polluting the whole community just as, in the proverbial saying, 'A little leaven leavens the whole lump'. Then, from the word 'leaven', St Paul's mind darts to the custom at Passover time of clearing from the house every bit of 'old leaven' and replacing it with new; and from the association of Passover time with the death of Jesus there comes to him the image of Jesus as the Paschal Lamb sacrificed on our behalf, purging from us 'the old leaven of malice and wickedness' and replacing it with 'the unleavened bread of sincerity and truth'. Is it not remarkable how swiftly St Paul's attention and thought pass from an instance of disgusting behaviour to the focal point or backcloth of all his thought – the story of Jesus Christ?

From the particularity of the story and for the preservation of its integrity, St Paul was as passionately concerned as he was for its dissemination to the ends of the earth, to all mankind. He heard once that in the churches of Galatia certain people were preaching a 'different gospel', telling a different story, perverting the good news of Christ; and that some of his own converts were attending to them. He himself wrote that he was 'astonished' to hear this, and we can tell from *what* he wrote that he was furious: he put a curse on anyone, even 'an angel from heaven', who perverted or distorted that which he himself had preached. But his fury did not arise out of an illusion that the good news of Christ was his own possession or out of resentment over the fact that others were, so to speak, invading his own territory. Far from it. St Paul's letter to his converts in the town of Philippi was written when he was in prison – probably in Rome – and his life in danger, and in this most affectionate and moving of all his letters he was delighted to tell his friends in Philippi that, though he was not able to preach the Gospel himself, his imprisonment was actually encouraging and advancing the preaching of the Gospel in the city. Some Christian brethren, knowing that he was in prison in defence of the Gospel, were themselves taking up his cause and his role out of love and loyalty. There were others, he admitted, who were doing so in a more competitive spirit and causing him pain as he lay helpless and useless in prison. But, he ended, what does this distinction of motives matter? Whatever the motive, the important thing is that all are telling the good news of Jesus Christ. The integrity of the story was much more important to St Paul than the person who told it: it was when this integrity was impaired or distorted that he was moved to anger.

In one of his letters to his rather troublesome converts in Corinth St Paul wrote these words: 'God was in Christ reconciling the world to himself, not counting their trespasses against them and entrusting to us the message of reconciliation.' These words report a particular event, something that has happened: they tell a story. They do not tell the story in full; they do not report all that the evangelists reported publicly in the market-places of the world and privately to people who wished to 'hear more' – they make no mention of the rejection of Jesus or his crucifixion or his resurrection from the dead. They are not misleading: they are true as far as they go. But they lack the *power* of meaning which can be received only by hearing and attending to the story itself – the full story of 'the things concerning Jesus'. Now of course the full story was already known to the Christians of Corinth and they would read St Paul's words in the light of what they already knew; and we are in the same position. So, speaking for myself, I find great comfort and encouragement in St Paul's words that in Christ God has already reconciled the world to himself, not counting our trespasses against us, and that he has entrusted to us the news of this reconciliation.

My contention in this chapter is, first, that the stories of particular events are, existentially, extremely important in our lives and experience; they affect us more powerfully, they 'mean more' to us, than general statements about the way the world is or what it ought to be; they have a *power* of meaning which cannot be conveyed and received otherwise than by attention to the story itself. My second contention is that our Christian religion came into the world, and took root in it, through the telling and receiving of the story of those particular events which are sometimes called 'the things concerning Jesus Christ'. It is that story which gave to Christianity its very existence – its 'power to be'. My next chapter will consist largely of stories of particular events in the world today in which there became evident the power of meaning of that story which the evangelists told in the market-places of the world of their day.

Chapter Three

THE SIGN OF THE CROSS

IN THE ANCIENT Saxon poem called *The Dream of the Rood* the unknown poet tells of a dream in which he or she encountered the actual cross on which Jesus was crucified and listened to its story. The cross told that once it had been a sapling growing on the wood edge, but when it reached maturity men came and hacked it down and dragged it away to a hilltop. There they hewed its branches into the form of a cross on which a criminal was to be put to death. 'But', said the cross, 'there came to me no criminal but the young hero, the Son of God;' and it told the poet how it trembled when he was raised up on it yet dared not bend under the weight, and how it was pierced by the nails driven through his hands and feet and drenched by the sweat of his agony and the blood from his wounds. It held him up for long hours, and when he died and his body was taken down for burial the cross itself was cut down and taken away and buried in a deep pit. But when he who had hung upon the cross was raised from death men came and uncovered the cross and raised it from the pit and decked it with gold and precious stones and paid great honour and respect to it and the last words which the poet hears from the cross are these: 'So now I tower high and mighty under the skies, having power to heal all who will bow before me.'

The image of the cross of Christ 'towering under the skies' would come quite naturally to the poet of long ago. In that age, and for many centuries afterwards, the Sign of the Cross hewn out of stone and often richly carved, was often set up for public view in the market-places of towns and on the skylines of the lonely countryside; it was raised up high to be a prominent feature both of townscapes and landscapes, and countless people must have looked up to it, and perhaps bowed before it, as they went about their business in towns or travelled slowly through miles of uninhabited country. In the world in which the old poet lived the cross of Christ must, literally, have 'towered under the skies'.

It does so no longer. Few medieval crosses survive for public view and of those which do some have become so eroded or vandalised that they are scarcely recognisable for what they are, and of course they have not been replaced by modern crosses at the centre of shopping malls or at busy road junctions or towering on the roofs of huge modern factories or the glittering palaces of commerce. Crosses have largely disappeared from public view. But this does not mean that crosses are no longer being made. A great many are being made – not of stone but of wood or metal, and these are small crosses, intended to be worn on a silver chain around someone's neck or placed at someone's bedside or put beside a photograph of some beloved person who has died or to be inscribed on the headstone of such a person's grave or perhaps to be set on the altar of a new church. One might say that in our age the Sign of the Cross has been removed from public view and 'taken indoors', or even that it has been 'privatised'.

But this does not mean that the cross of Christ has lost its power to heal – whether it be in the form of an ancient stone cross still recognisable as such, or a wooden cross at a bedside or a cross of palm leaves received in church on Palm Sunday. Once in my life I encountered this power for myself and, having done so, I have been alert to remember the effects of this healing power of which I have been told or which I have observed for myself. For the rest of this chapter I have chosen six stories, beginning with my own, of the encounters with the healing power of the cross of Christ of people of different backgrounds and in different circumstances.

In the early years of my ministry there was a longish period when it was not possible to take any kind of holiday away from my parish. As time went on I became rather resentful of the situation and sorry for myself, but eventually circumstances changed and I arranged to spend a week with friends who lived close to the sea in West Wales. However, shortly before my holiday was due to begin, circumstances changed again and the holiday had to be cut down to three days, and I was not at all pleased. But I went to my friends, and the first day at the coast was perfectly lovely – sunshine, peace, the wide sea, birds around the cliff, the smell of heather, the kindness of my host and hostess, everything. However, when the post arrived the following morning my host handed me a letter addressed to me in the handwriting of one of the officials of my church. I presumed it would contain a note of good wishes for a pleasant holiday.

But it did not. It contained a long, petulant series of complaints originating in an incident that must have happened within an hour or two of my leaving home and extending much beyond that. My pent-up self-pity erupted and blazed: I was furious with the writer, with the woman who had been responsible for the incident, even with my innocent hosts for handing me such a letter. I was furious with everyone – with people in general: could they not leave me alone even for *three days*? I said curtly to my host, 'I am going for a walk' and strode out of the house towards the shore where at that time of day there would be few, if any, people; and then remembering that nearby there was a long, narrow promontory which stretched two miles or so out to sea, I made for that. I was certain that at the far end of that, the headland, there would be no people at all. Not till I got to the headland – as far away as possible from people – would I try to calm down and compose myself. I walked head-down, noticing nothing of the sea and birds and heather around me. I walked fast – like Tam o' Shanter in Robbie Burns' poem, 'Gathering my brows like a gathering storm, nursing my wrath to keep it warm' – and it was not long before I could see waves breaking over the headland no more than a couple of hundred yards ahead. But I never reached the headland; for, as I rounded the last outcrop of rock, I suddenly saw, slightly to the right of my path and no more than two or three yards away, a large, black, stone cross. I do not know to this day by whom it was set up, or when or for what reason, but it stopped me in my tracks. The path carried on beyond it but I could not. The cross held me in front of it for a few seconds not so much bowing as cowering; and then it turned me to the right and sent me back along the path by which I had come – back to where people were. But it sent me back a different man. It was as if it had pricked the balloon of my self-pity or lanced the carbuncle of my anger and drained the foul pus. I do not know *what* it meant to me: no intellectual activity went on in me during the seconds in which I stood before it. But, whatever it meant, the power of its meaning healed me, and on my way back to my host's house I was delighted to chat with any people I met.

Sometime after this encounter with the Sign of the Cross I was chatting in the refreshment room of a railway station with three or four men who, like me, were waiting for a long overdue train. We were all strangers to one another but of similar age, and conversation naturally turned to what we had been doing in the last war. It turned out that one of us was a German, but his English was good and the rest of us listened with interest to what he had to say. He told us that he had been in the German Army on the eastern front, had been taken prisoner by the Russians and had been held for a long time in one of their prisoner of war camps in Siberia. Someone remarked that this must have been a 'pretty grim' experience. The German replied, 'Yes, it was not good,' but then he added, 'there were *some* things that were good: I should like to tell you of one of them.' The story which the German told us was this. One day in the camp he had found a *whole* cigarette, and this promised so great a treat that he looked for an opportunity to light and smoke it undisturbed. In the corner of the camp there was a rubbish-dump in which a fire was always smouldering. It was out of bounds to the prisoners, but he resolved to slip away there unobserved, light his cigarette at the fire and smoke it there before his absence was noticed. He did slip away and light his cigarette, but unfortunately a Russian guard had observed what he did. The Russian came up quietly behind him, struck him on the head with the butt of his rifle and knocked him to the ground. As the German lay on his back, stunned and helpless, he saw the Russian fix his bayonet and hold it pointed to strike at his heart. To the prisoners the Russian guards were 'laws unto themselves', and the German thought that for his breach of the rules he was about to pay with his life. He had been brought up as a Catholic and had a distant memory that one should, if possible, make the Sign of the Cross at the moment of death. He did so, and closed his eyes. But nothing happened. When he opened his eyes he saw the Russian withdraw the bayonet, turn on his heel and go away. The German managed to get on to his feet and stood there for a little while trying to pull himself together before returning to his fellow-prisoners. Then he saw the Russian coming back again but this time he had a glass of milk in his hand, and gave it to the German. Then he took two cigarettes from his pocket: one he gave to the German and lit for him, the other he lit for himself. Neither man could speak or understand the other's language, but the Russian sat down on a log and beckoned to the German to sit beside him. So, until their cigarettes were finished, the two men sat side by side smiling and nodding to each other.

The German ended his story by saying, 'I think that was good', and we who heard it agreed. One does not know what the Sign of the Cross meant to the Russian, but whatever it meant was so powerful that for a little while it overcame in that grim camp the huge barriers of language and status and national enmity which lay between the prison guard and the prisoner.

The third story also involves a soldier – a member of the Parachute Regiment of the British Army. He was aged 23, happily married and the father of a little daughter. In the autumn of 1970 he fell ill, and investigations by Army doctors revealed – to their shock and distress – that he (his name was Ken) was suffering from cancer so widely spread that it was, 25 years ago, beyond any form of treatment by surgery or any other form of medication. They told Ken frankly of his condition; and he asked them that he might be sent home to be nursed by his wife for as long as possible. The Army doctors readily agreed, and, what is more, they posted a team of three Army nurses to the vicinity of Ken's home so that one of them should be in his home 24 hours a day to help his wife with the nursing and, in particular, to give the three-hourly injection of heroin which was already necessary to ease his pain.

Ken was brought home just in time for Christmas, and his home was in my parish. But it was only recently that he and his family had moved there and few of the neighbours knew them, so it was several weeks before I heard of Ken's sad condition. By then he was very ill indeed – lying in bed flat on his back, dreadfully emaciated and scarcely able to speak. I did not think it right to offer the challenge or comfort of religion to one who, literally, could not answer back: so my colleague or I used simply to call each day and sit by his bed for a few minutes and say a few friendly things and tell him how brave he was being. We noticed that the relief of each three-hourly injection of heroin lasted only two hours and a half. Then the agony returned, showing itself in the sweat on his hands and face, and Ken's eyes moved slowly to the electric clock on the wall and stayed fixed there as he watched the minutes pass ever so slowly towards the time of his next easement and relief.

On the evening of Palm Sunday I had a palm cross in my pocket. By then Ken could not speak at all, and I did not wish to thrust on him anything to which he could not genuinely assent. So I simply showed him the cross and explained that we had all received one in church that morning because during the week we should be remembering Jesus dying for our sake. 'This cross is mine,' I said, 'and when I get home

I shall pin it up in my house. But if you or your wife would like a cross in your house you are very welcome to this one – I can easily get another for myself. If you would like to have it, just nod your head, will you, Ken.' Ken did not nod his head, but ever so slowly he raised both his hands and took the cross and placed it in his pyjama pocket. During the next few days I noticed that as each recurring half-hour of agony began Ken would move his right arm across his chest and take hold of his cross.

When I called on the evening of Good Friday his wife asked me to come into the kitchen first and join her in a cup of tea. 'We've had such a strange day,' she said, 'this morning he wouldn't settle. He kept moving his right hand and arm about as if he was trying to push something away. I thought he was seeing something in the room that was offending him and I moved just about everything there was. But that made no difference, and I felt so guilty that I couldn't help him when he needed me. And then I suddenly noticed that, when nurse had changed his pyjamas this morning she had forgotten to put the cross into his clean pair. So I fetched it and put it where it belonged, and since then he's been . . . Well, you'll see for yourself how he is when we go in.' So we went into the front room where Ken was lying quite still with his right arm across his chest and his hand holding on to his cross. And so he remained until he died just at noon on Easter Monday.

I do not know what the Sign of the Cross meant to this young paratrooper; by the time he received it he *could* not tell me – he could not speak at all. But whatever it meant it must have meant very powerfully – so powerfully that when other comforts, including the comfort of heroin, failed him he groped for his cross and, having found it, held it until he died.

My fourth story is of an incident which happened in the same parish as the third. The church with the vicarage beside it stood at the top of a small hill, and the east ends of the two buildings were widely visible from the majority of the roads and houses of the parish; and the east end of the vicarage, a gable end, was a blank brick wall. One year, as Good Friday approached, a suggestion was made that on that wall a large cross should be raised up on the Saturday before Good Friday and illuminated by floodlights until the following Saturday. The suggestion was welcomed by the church council, and a wooden cross, some twelve feet high and painted white, was constructed and set up on the wall on the day suggested. On the evening of that day, when dusk fell and the floodlights came on, I walked down to the bottom of the road which led directly up to the church and vicarage to see the visual effects of the cross. In the darkness they were impressive: against the background of the brick wall the white cross seemed almost to be floating in the air. Though darkness had fallen it was not yet the time when people go out on Saturday evenings, and the streets were perfectly quiet, so I had the chance to reflect on what we had done. Certainly it was visually effective and, in that sense, successful; but I wondered if it would have any more significant effect.

Then the figure of a man came into my view: he walked briskly out of a side-street only a few yards in front of me and turned to the left to continue in the direction of the church. I recognised him at once: he was a labourer with the Water Board but, sad to say, a notoriously 'hard man' who became violent when he drank too much and was the instigator of many fights in pubs and crises at home. As I say, he turned to go in the direction of the church and I could see his figure silhouetted against the floodlights. After a few steps he suddenly stopped. Obviously he had seen the cross and its unexpected appearance had startled him: it would startle anyone who saw it for the first time, seeming as it did to float in the air. He remained still for a few moments. Then he took his cap off. Then he set off again to continue up the hill, but now he walked not briskly but slowly, stiffly, almost like someone sleep-walking. He continued to the top of the road; then he stepped on to the grass which lay around the church and vicarage and walked across it until he came to the foot of the cross. There he knelt down, and from where I stood his bareheaded figure was just within the aureole of the light which was focused upon the cross. He was still kneeling there when a few minutes later I returned quietly to the vicarage.

I never told him what I had seen on that night: to have done so would have been an invasion of his privacy – almost a kind of blackmail. So I have no idea what the Sign of the Cross meant to that 'hard man'. But, whatever it meant, its meaning must have been very powerful – so powerful that it moved him, quite 'out of character', to an act of piety and respect unusual in our society. He was a Lancastrian: and Lancastrian men in particular are very averse to 'wearing their religion on their sleeve'.

The next story was told me in a church near Liverpool at which I had been asked to preach on Good Friday. In my sermon I had referred several times to the healing power of the Sign of the Cross. After the service the vicar told me that a man in the congregation wished to have a word with me – a sea captain, the vicar said, whose ship had been the first British ship to pick up 'boat people' fleeing from Vietnam. He introduced me to the captain, whose courteous yet authoritative manner was just as I would have expected in a man of his profession. 'Padre', he said when the vicar left us together, 'what you said in your sermon about the power of the cross is perfectly true. I have seen it for myself.' Then he told me his story, which was about his encounter with the boat-people. When they were sighted their boat was drifting around with no power at all, and when he sent some of his crew to inspect the situation they found the boat waterlogged and its occupants without food or water and suffering severely from exposure. They were also terrified of the ship's crew, having no common language and fearing that the crew had come to arrest them and take them back to Vietnam. The Captain ordered that they should be persuaded to leave their hulk and be brought to his ship in its lifeboat, and in the meantime he had the after-deck of the ship cleared, hot food prepared and blankets and similar coverings collected for the boat-peoples' use. The process of persuasion took a long time and when the boat-people were brought aboard ship they were still terrified. The Captain said that his men were 'very good' in smiling and nodding and gesturing to their 'guests': but to no avail. The unfortunate people fled and huddled together on one part of the deck and, if any of the crew went near them, fled again together to another; and if the crew got out of the way they would come no nearer to the food and coverings left for them but remained in their huddle. 'I was at my wit's end, Padré . . . and then I had an idea. I sent for my carpenter, Bill, and told him to get some timber and put it together as a large cross and set it up where our guests couldn't help seeing it. He did that, Padré, and it worked. Very soon they were taking the food, and I left them to get on with it. Before I turned in that night I went on deck to see that they were all right: I found them all under blankets sleeping around Bill's cross. I was rather moved, Padré. Next day we put them ashore at a safe haven. So what you said in your sermon was right, Padré.'

Obviously, the Captain, having no knowledge of his guests' language, did not know what the Sign of the Cross meant to them; but clearly its meaning was powerful enough to reassure them when the well-meant smiles and gestures of his ship's crew were powerless to do so.

The sixth story was told me by a nun of great age when she was reminiscing about her early days in community when she was still a novice and scarcely more than a girl. She belonged then to a community which was dwindling in numbers and for which their convent was becoming unnecessarily large. When a smaller and more suitable property not very far away was put up for sale the possibility of moving there was mooted among the sisters: obviously it was a rather unwelcome possibility to sisters for whom the present convent had been their home for fifty or even sixty years. Discussions went on for a long time; and eventually the owner of the property, who was holding it at a price which was acceptable to the sisters, told them that he had another client who was interested in it and must have their decision by a certain date.

So the sisters met to make their decision, and after earnest prayer for guidance each in turn was asked to tell her preference. All except one – a lady of strong personality who was the treasurer – opted for moving to the other property and the treasurer was asked to tell the owner of their decision.

But the following morning the novice – whom I will call

Mary – was quietly dusting in the library when she overheard
the treasurer speaking on the telephone. She was telling the
owner of the property, clearly and beyond all doubt, that
the community did *not* wish to move there. Mary was bewildered: how could the treasurer have made such a mistake?
She went timidly to the treasurer and told her what she had
overheard; but all she received in return was a rebuke for her
impertinence in, as a Novice, presuming to correct so senior
a member of the community. She was dismissed with, as the
saying goes, 'a flea in her ear'. What should Mary now do?
Her dilemma was painful. Should she, a mere newcomer,
make known to the mother or anyone else what she had
heard and so poison the atmosphere of the community?
Should she, could she, remain in community with a sister
who had so betrayed the community and flouted its wishes?
Could she herself leave the community without explanation
of her reason for doing so or without telling lies about her
reason? Her problem obsessed her: for days she could neither
eat nor sleep nor pray and she performed her physical duties
like a zombie. Eventually out of sheer exhaustion she fell
asleep one afternoon in a chair, and in her troubled sleep
had a dream. She dreamed that she was trying to climb a
steep and slippery bank. She knew that she *had* to climb it
for some unknown reason, but each time she neared the top
she slipped backwards and had to start again. So it went on;
but eventually she reached the top, and there she found a
large cross standing, and she took hold of it, and she knew
that she had done what she had to and that all was well.

Then Mary woke up; and in her wakened life all was still
well. Her obsession was gone and her problem became of no
importance. Sixty years or so later, when Sister Mary told
me this story, she was a distinguished theologian and a very

———

experienced counsellor; and she pointed out to me that it was not surprising that, in such a situation, she should have had such a dream. What was surprising – or at any rate significant – was that her dream-encounter with the cross should have such power in her waking life. She pointed out that from the dream-cross she had received no specific guidance or advice about her problem and its solution: it simply assured her that 'all is well', and this assurance reduced her obsessive problem to triviality. When I asked her what actually happened afterwards – what she did or did not do – she could no longer remember: all she could tell me was that somehow 'things got sorted out'. So here again we cannot say exactly what the Sign of the Cross meant to young Mary; all we can say is that its power of meaning was enough to lift her obsession and reduce her problem to small proportions.

In all these stories the Sign of the Cross had power to heal – heal anger and enmity and obsession and so on. But I do not for a moment wish to give the impression that its power is 'miraculous' or 'magical' in the sense in which those words were used in the Middle Ages of alleged fragments of the 'true cross' which were then being marketed around Christendom. The power of the Sign of the Cross is derived entirely from the story of the cross and of him who died upon it. To anyone who knows nothing of the story of the cross the Sign means *nothing* – it is merely an object of a certain shape. Years ago, just after the war, I worked briefly for an organisation with the curious name of the Cambridge Hopping Mission. Its purpose was to provide basic services and amenities for thousands of families from London's East End who migrated into Kent in the early autumn to harvest the hops. They had to live in rather squalid conditions, and among the services we provided were first-aid stations in the form of bell-tents, and in the one in which I worked someone had attached a crucifix to the central pole. One morning three boys aged about twelve arrived: they had been picking blackberries and had acquired a good many cuts and scratches. I patched them up to their satisfaction and as they went out of the tent and I attended to the next 'patient' they noticed the crucifix and I overheard what they said in their rich Cockney accent. 'Who's that?' asked the first: 'I don't know,' said the second. 'It's what's his name . . . Jesus,' answered the third, and then they were off. It was unusual at that date to meet with children of the boys' age who were so ignorant of even the rudiments of Christian teaching; and the incident has stuck in my mind. It is sad to think those lively boys – or at least two of them – were likely to go through life deprived of the possibility of being healed by the Sign of the Cross in their times of need; and it is sadder still to reflect that thousands of children today are equally deprived.

Chapter Four

THE GRACE OF JESUS CHRIST

THE PREVIOUS CHAPTER illustrated the healing power of the story of Jesus in the world of today. When certain people who knew the story were reminded of it by the sight of a cross they were powerfully affected, uplifted, changed, healed. They did not, and could not, put into words what the story meant to them at that moment; they did not, and could not, define its meaning. But they found themselves deeply affected by it: they understood and received and were healed by what the story 'said' to them.

As we saw in the second chapter, the meaning of a story can be received only from the story itself; it cannot be distilled or encapsulated adequately in statements or summaries of 'what the story means'. Nevertheless we can help one another to understand what the story means. Just as a teacher can help students to understand what a poem means, so we can help one another to understand what the story of Jesus – or any other story – means. We can draw the attention of others to details within the story, to contrasts within it, to the resonances of particular words and phrases; we can draw attention too to 'silences' within the story – to facts or incidents of which the story makes no mention. The purpose of this chapter is to do this – to draw attention to details within the story of Jesus which strike me as significant and which others may perhaps find helpful.

We have, of course, received the story of Jesus from the writings of Matthew, Mark, Luke and John. It was they who filled out, from their own memories or from what they had heard from contemporaries, the good news of Jesus which had been proclaimed so briefly and succinctly by the first evangelists; and by putting the story 'on paper' they made it available to the generations yet to come. But we must make a distinction between the purposes of the four writers. The sole purpose of Matthew, Mark and Luke was to record the particularities of events in the life of Jesus; but John had the further purpose of stating the enduring meaning of those events. Whereas Matthew, Mark and Luke simply told the story of Jesus, John included within the framework of the story statements of the enduring meaning of the story. The first three writers let the story speak for itself and make its own impact on the reader: John, who was almost certainly the last of the four to put the story 'on paper', offered to the reader, within the framework of the story, an interpretation of its meaning which became, and still remains, the foundation-stone of Christian theology.

John's interpretation of the meaning of the story of Jesus is presented in the first sentences that he wrote:

> In the beginning was the Word, and the Word was with God, and the Word was God. He was in the beginning with God: all things were made by him and without him was not any-thing made that was made . . . He was in the world and the world was made by him and the world knew him not . . . The Word was made flesh and dwelt among us and we beheld his glory, the glory as of the only begotten of the Father.

John stated in his opening words the unique status, the divine identity, of Jesus; and as he continued he constantly referred to Jesus claiming or asserting or drawing attention to his own status and identity. John attributed to Jesus, especially when he was alone with his disciples, long homilies in which he spoke of himself as 'the bread of life', 'the light of the world', 'the way, the truth and the life', 'the resurrection and the life', 'the one by whom alone people may come to the Father'; John wrote of Jesus as of one whose primary concern when he dwelt among us was that people should recognise him for who he was and trust in him alone for guidance and peace and salvation.

So John's purpose was not simply to record the particularities of Jesus' life – the things he did and said and suffered: it was also to state, in memorable and majestic terms, who it was who so acted and spoke and suffered. In John's writing the story of Jesus was only the framework within which he expressed and interpreted the enduring meaning, the significance for all mankind, of Jesus' life among us. In this sense the story told by Matthew, Mark and Luke was marginalised by John. It was not ignored or contradicted, but it occupied less space than in the works of the other writers and contained less of the details of what actually happened in the life of Jesus.

So it is in the writings of Matthew, Mark and Luke that I find most of the details which appeal to me as calling for particular attention. The first, recorded by Luke, is Jesus' encounter with Zacchaeus the Publican. In the years when I used to teach children in Sunday School I found that the story of this incident was by far the most popular with the children of all the stories which I had to tell. As soon as I mentioned the name 'Zacchaeus' children who had heard the story before would smile and draw their chairs a little nearer, and when we reached the denouement there were smiles again – sometimes accompanied by eyes on the edge of tears or lumps in throats. Jesus treated the 'poor little rich man' just as children themselves long to be treated when they have misbehaved and are in misery and disgrace. Jesus relieved Zacchaeus of his burden of guilt and shame just as wise and understanding parents relieve the misery of their naughty children. Jesus did not say to Zacchaeus 'I forgive you for your misdeeds' – still less did he say 'I will forgive you if you apologise for your misdeeds and promise to mend your ways.' Jesus healed and saved Zacchaeus by asking a kindness of him – his hospitality for the night. So it is that understanding parents heal the shame and misery of their children when they misbehave – by asking a small kindness of them such as calling the cat in or 'fetching my glasses from upstairs'. I remember from my own childhood and its times of shame and misery how welcome was such a request and how gladly and eagerly I did what was asked of me: and so it was with Zacchaeus – he 'hastened down' from his perch on the tree and he received Jesus 'gladly' at his home.

It is extraordinary that until we received the Alternative Service Book we never heard the story of Jesus and Zacchaeus read as the gospel for the day. For it is a vivid and powerful illustration of the meaning of Paul's statement 'God was in Christ reconciling the world to himself, not counting their trespasses against them and entrusting to us the message of reconciliation.' It shows us a concrete instance of God in Christ 'not counting' a man's trespasses and reconciling that man to himself. Zacchaeus was notorious as a trespasser or sinner, and so was a social outcast; and Jesus by his initiative reconciled him to God and man. In the story we read of

Jesus 'not counting against him' Zacchaeus's trespasses: he made no mention of them. He treated them as if they did not exist and simply asked him for his hospitality as a man might ask a friend. Jesus healed or 'won back' – that is to say 'redeemed' – this man whose shameful behaviour had estranged him from God and man; and he did so by treating him as still 'one of us', as still a friend of whom a kindness might be asked and received.

In the story of Jesus and Zacchaeus there is no mention of 'forgiveness' on the part of Jesus or of 'repentance' on the part of Zacchaeus. As we saw in the second chapter, the words 'I forgive you' can be very unattractive to hear – even repulsive. Though we approve of forgiveness as a virtue we find that existentially, in close encounters with explicit words of forgiveness, we often feel 'put down', humiliated and resentful. We often want and need the forgiveness of someone to whom, through our carelessness or selfishness, we have caused inconvenience or given offence: we often apologise and ask for forgiveness. But decent people, thoughtful people – indeed *most* people – will respond not with formal words of forgiveness or conditional forgiveness but with a smile and a joke, a bit of banter, a kiss or warm handshake or a request to 'put this in the post for me on the way home' or 'give me a lift to the station'. It is by this *manner* of forgiveness that forgiveness is made welcome and gladly received and reconciles us to one another.

We notice also in the story of Jesus and Zacchaeus that it was not through Zacchaeus's repentance that he won Jesus' unspoken but welcome forgiveness. It was Jesus who initiated by the *manner* of his forgiveness the reconciliation of this 'poor little rich man' and won from him that change of mind and outlook which Jesus called his 'salvation'. The story of this incident in Jesus life is surely of great significance: it presents to us a shining example of the *grace* of our Lord Jesus Christ – of his speaking and acting in such a way that people were attracted by him and welcomed his presence and responded to him with gratitude and joy.

Throughout the story of Jesus we read of many occasions on which Jesus spoke about our need for forgiveness and our duty of forgiving. In the prayer which he taught to his disciples they were to ask their Father in heaven 'to forgive us our trespasses as we forgive those who trespass against us'. To Peter who asked him how often he should forgive an offending brother he replied, in effect, 'Not seven times but times without number'. People who came to him for healing or help were often told by him that their sins were forgiven. On the cross he prayed, 'Father, forgive them for they know not what they do'; and he said that he himself, the son of man, had authority on earth to forgive. But never in the story do we read of Jesus saying to anyone 'I forgive you'. He did not say it even when, as the risen Lord, he encountered Peter full of guilt and shame for his disloyalty: he asked of Peter that he would undertake the role of 'shepherd of the flock', and in *this* manner forgave him. In his words and works of forgiveness Jesus never asserted or implied his own moral superiority over the sinner; he never left the offender with an unwelcome, uncomfortable sense of his or her own inferiority. He forgave in such a way that the sinful person was *reconciled*, relieved of guilt and shame, at ease with himself or herself, at peace with others. By his considerateness of the sinful person's feelings, by his understanding of that person's point of view, he created that situation which in the Sanscrit language was called *gurtas* – the situation of grace in which what is offered is welcome and naturally evokes gratitude and joy.

Now let us attend to the manner in which Jesus carried out his works of physical and mental healing which occupy so much space in the story of Jesus. For three years they were high on Jesus' agenda. Many sick or demented people came or were brought to him in hope of healing and in some cases he went when asked to someone's house. No one was rejected by him – not even when on the Sabbath he was engaged in preaching in the synagogue, nor when determined friends of a paralysed man opened the roof of a house to lay the patient at Jesus' feet. We must notice not only that Jesus never turned away a person who sought his healing but also that he never *laid down conditions* on which he would exercise his healing power – he never 'bargained' with would-be patients in such terms as 'I will heal you if you will promise to mend your ways' or 'If I heal you, will you become my follower?' Nor did Jesus seek to bind to himself those whom he healed – to put them under a sense of obligation to him. It is true that Mary Magdalene, out of whom he had 'driven seven devils', became his devoted follower; but of most of those who were healed by him we read that Jesus 'sent them home', asking them in some cases to 'tell no one' of what had happened and in other cases 'to praise God' for their healing, and sometimes telling them that it was 'by their own faith' that they were healed. The healing of Jesus was a free gift which enlarged rather than restricted the freedom of those who received it: he exercised his power to heal so quietly and gently and unobtrusively that the rumour spread by certain opponents – that it was the demonic power of the prince of devils – did not deter people in need of healing from seeking it from Jesus. Even the opponents of Jesus could not convince people that his power to heal contained any kind of threat. Jesus' works of healing were works of grace – welcome to those who needed them and naturally evoking gratitude and joy.

As I have said, works of healing were high on Jesus' agenda. Higher still came preaching and teaching. Mark wrote that after Jesus' baptism and his time of solitude in the wilderness he 'came into Galilee preaching the good news of God and saying "The time is fulfilled and the kingdom of God is at hand: repent and believe in the good news." ' Let me draw attention again to what I have written before – that the Greek word which is translated into English as 'repent' does *not* mean 'regret and confess your sins and mend your ways': it means 'see things in a new light and respond accordingly'. In Jesus' preaching he told the good news of God, and called on people to see things in the light of this good news and to respond accordingly; and Mark goes on to tell of his preaching in the synagogue in Capernaum and the astonishment of those present at the authority with which he spoke. Jesus preached *about* God with a confidence which impressed his hearers, but he did not preach *as* God. He had received at his baptism a vision, a revelation, an insight, that he was the beloved son of God; but never in the story of Jesus do we read of him saying that he was *the* only son of God or that he was God himself. On the contrary, he consistently referred to himself as 'son of man'; and in referring to God as '*your* Father in heaven' he clearly implied that *all* sons and daughters of men were sons and daughters of God. In the society in which Jesus lived the claim of anyone actually 'to be God' or to be unique as 'Son of God' would have been repulsive, a mark of madness or a demonic blasphemy. Jesus preaching made no such claim, and to many of those who heard it was attractive and welcome.

In his preaching and teaching about God Jesus often challenged or fell foul of the teaching of the accepted religious leaders of his day. He criticised their pedantry – their insistence on the minute particulars of the law of Moses as they interpreted it. They laid down in precise detail what the law of Moses required of people and what it forbade: they prescribed exactly how far one might walk on the Sabbath without breaking it, how exactly one must cleanse pots and vessels before eating or drinking from them, and so on. Jesus challenged their teaching in such words as 'They bind heavy burdens, hard to bear, and lay them on men's shoulders, and they themselves will not move them with a finger', 'they have neglected the weightier matters of the law – justice and mercy and faith' and, when he and his disciples were accused of breaking the Sabbath, he said to them 'the Sabbath was made for man; not man for the Sabbath' and 'Is it lawful on the Sabbath to do good or to do harm, to save life or to kill?' Jesus brought the good news that God is not *burdensome*, and the 'repentance' for which he asked was that mankind should 'see' God, and speak and think of God, in this new light. So he said, 'Come to me, all who labour and are heavy laden and I will give you rest. Take my yoke upon you and learn from me; for I am gentle and lowly in heart and you will find rest for your souls. For my yoke is easy and my burden light.' By comparison with the burden of duties and restrictions imposed by other religious teachers of his day the burden of Jesus' teaching was indeed 'light'. He encouraged people to think of God as 'our Father in heaven' who knows our human needs for such mundane essentials as food and clothing and relieves our natural but sometimes obsessive anxieties over such matters; who, like a human father, will not give a serpent to a child who asks for an egg: who, like a good neighbour, will eventually come to the door if we persist in knocking in the middle of the night; who, like the father of the Prodigal Son, will run to welcome the errant young man when he comes home reluctantly in shame and disgrace. Such 'homely' images of God which Jesus presented in his teaching must have been attractive and welcome to many of those who heard him and received by many with gratitude and gladness. Jesus' teaching about God was full of grace.

Much of that teaching was, of course, expressed in Jesus' parables. It is often supposed that Jesus 'made up' his parables in order to convey moral or theological truth to simple people. It seems to me very unlikely that this was the case. For three years Jesus was moving about the villages of Galilee and Judaea meeting and talking with all kinds of people, receiving hospitality from some and criticism from others, healing many, approachable to all, exposed to all. He lived very close to people and was very interested in and observant of the world in which people lived. To the disciples who were usually with him he often remarked on the ways of parents with their children and of children playing in the market-place; of farmers sowing their seed and of shepherds in whose flock one sheep was missing. He referred to the effects of putting new wine into old bottles and leaven into a lump of dough and to the fact that rain falls equally on 'the just and the unjust'; he drew the attention of his disciples to a poor widow emptying her thin purse into the treasury of the Temple, to a fig tree bearing no fruit and to the beauty of the 'lilies of the field'. It is surely improbable that one so perceptive of what is going on in the world would *need* to 'make up' those stories which we call his parables. Surely it is more likely that, for instance, he had actually overheard the prayers of a Pharisee and a publican in the Temple; that a woman had told him of her distress at losing a coin, of the way she 'swept the house' to find it and of her delight when she found it; that someone – perhaps several people – had told him of the exceptional kindness which a Samaritan had shown to a man who had been 'mugged' on his way from Jerusalem to Jericho; that he himself had been present in a market-place when there was a dispute between day-labourers and their employer about fair pay. Only one of Jesus' many parables *must* have been made up – that of Dives and Lazarus, of which the setting was not in this world but in the next; but it was not necessarily made up by Jesus. It seems much more likely from its setting and its tone, that it was a parable told by rabbis and repeated by Jesus on some occasion when a poor man or a poor woman was being treated or spoken of with contempt.

Scarcely distinguishable from the parables of Jesus are the metaphors and similes which he used in his teaching about God and the kingdom of God. He taught that God feeds the birds and knows when a sparrow dies and clothes the grass of the field and counts the hairs on every human head. He likened the kingdom of God to a grain of seed which grows into a bush in which birds can roost and to a touch of leaven which swells a whole loaf. He spoke of those who listened to his teaching as 'the salt of the earth' which must not lose its taste, as 'the light of the world' which is not to be put under a cover but to shine throughout the house, as 'a city set on a hill which cannot be hid'. He called on his followers to be 'as wise as serpents and innocent as doves'; he urged them not to display their generosity by 'sounding a trumpet' but to keep even their own left hand unaware of what their right hand was giving; he warned them against attempting to remove a speck from a brother's eye when there was a log in their own eye; he advised them to 'beware of false prophets who come to you in sheep's clothing but inwardly are ravenous wolves'.

The manner of Jesus' teaching about God was very 'down to earth' – one might even say 'homely'. His stories and similes and metaphors were drawn from the world in which he lived and which was familiar to his hearers. Though we hear occasionally from Matthew, Mark and Luke that he preached in the formal setting of a synagogue it is evident that for the most part his teaching was given out of doors, at the lakeside or the top of a hill or in a market-place, or sometimes in a house in which he was receiving hospitality. It is evident too that, though some people came to him to seek his healing for themselves or their friends and others to criticise him or oppose his teaching, the majority were *drawn* to him by the manner of his teaching. They found it attractive and welcome – unlike in this respect the teaching of the recognised religious teachers known as scribes. It is a platitude that 'children loves stories'; it is also true that children are very sensitive to stories and moved to tears by stories with 'unhappy endings'. And this sensitivity is not confined to children. As we have seen stories have a *power* of meaning which is lacking in general statements: they are more *interesting* than statements, more 'hearer-friendly' and more likely to remain in the hearer's memory. Jesus' manner of teaching about God and about the kingdom of God – full of stories and vivid metaphors and similes – was 'hearer-friendly'. It *drew* people to listen and attend, and it drew them the more, no doubt, because for the most part Jesus taught in informal circumstances in which anyone could come and go and raise questions and comments and criticisms. The *homely* manner in which he taught about God and his kingdom was, and still is, a lovely instance or illustration of the grace of our Lord Jesus Christ.

Now of course, there was another side or aspect to Jesus' teaching. To his closest followers he told not only the good news of God but also what they must be prepared for in the world. He taught them not only that the kingdom of God was 'among them' in the world but also that they must pray to God 'Thy kingdom come'. He likened the kingdom of God to a tiny seed which *eventually* becomes a shrub in which birds roost and a pinch of leaven which *in time* swells the whole loaf. He said, in effect, that the dawn has indeed broken but that the world has not yet recognised it as the dawn. So his disciples must be prepared to live and indeed to suffer in a world still living in darkness. They must be prepared to bear witness to the good news of God in a world still sceptical – still disbelieving that 'the grace of God has dawned upon the world with healing for all mankind'. They must expect to encounter, in the future as in the past, wars in the world, natural disaster, divisions and conflicts within families and communities, and, for themselves, opposition to the truth to which they bore witness and persecution for what they said and did. He said to them 'He that endureth to the end shall be saved'. He taught them to be, in the troubled and often cruel world, ever faithful and ever loyal to the good news of God which he himself had preached.

I cannot believe, as some Christians do believe, that Jesus, being the Son of God, was endowed with a unique foreknowledge of the future – including the foreknowledge that he would die as he did in Jerusalem and on the third day be raised from death. If he had this foreknowledge his death, though painful, would have been attended by a confidence and comfort denied to mortal men, and his words upon the cross both of forgiveness and of dereliction would be no more than charades. I cannot help believing what St Paul wrote – that when the Son of God came among us he 'emptied himself and was made in the likeness of man'. He knew only as human beings know. When he was baptised by John he received, as many men and women have received, a *calling*. He became aware, as many men and women have become aware, that God had a particular purpose for him; and that purpose was that he should make known in the world the good news of God. He did, as many men and women have done, what he believed God would have him do: and as he did it he found himself endowed with certain gifts and powers which are unusual among mankind. Other men and women have found themselves so endowed as they followed their calling: other men and women, from St Paul onwards, have found themselves *inspired* as they fulfilled God's purpose for them.

But such people, and Jesus also, have, in St Paul's words, 'walked by faith not by sight'. Their gifts have not included foreknowledge. In my book, *Love's Endeavour, Love's Expense* (Darton, Longman and Todd, 1977), I have suggested that God himself does not know in advance the future of his creation. I have likened God to a great artist who, in painting a picture, does not know in advance, does not '*see*' in advance, the picture which he or she is painting. The artist is constantly standing back from the painting, watching how it is 'coming on', toning down a colour which is too bright in the context of other colours around it, correcting a curve or brush-stroke which, as the picture develops, is becoming too prominent, introducing a figure or a shape which is seen to be necessary as the picture comes near to completion. The creator of the picture, the great artist, is ever working towards the completion of a great picture; but he or she does not 'foreknow' the corrections and adjustments and alterations which will be necessary in the progress of the work as it moves towards the final brush-stroke and the completion and fulfilment of the artist's endeavour.

If this analogy between God and the creative artist has any validity we cannot possibly think of Jesus as knowing the world's future and his own future with crystal clarity – as if he could look forward into future time as astronomers look through telescopes into the immensities of space. When he prepared his close followers for their future he did so not as a clairvoyant but as a thoughtful realist and so he did also when he spoke to them of his own future. At the beginning of his ministry he found himself called to be a 'messenger-of-good-news' – good news of what God is like and of the manner in which the kingdom of God will come and God's will be done on earth as it is in heaven. Jesus not only preached and taught the good news in parables and metaphors and similes: he also enacted it in the world in which he lived – in his quiet and gentle healing of the sick or handicapped who came to him; in his easing of burdens of guilt which some people bore; in his ready accessibility to young and old, to friend and stranger, to decent people and to notorious sinners; in his lifestyle which exposed him both to hospitality and to rebuff; in his informality which not only made him popular but also laid him open to criticism and contempt.

Jesus was, of course, brought up as a Jew. He must have been well aware of the history of his nation and in particular of the words and works of those who had been messengers from God in the past – the prophets. They had suffered in various ways – some, like Jeremiah, physically at the hands of the authorities who took offence at their pessimism, others mentally in the frustration and anger and even despair to which they were reduced by the indifference of the nation to their messages. It was to and for the nation that the prophets spoke or wrote. They did not target individuals but rebuked *the nation* for its infidelity to God or indifference to God's law, or offered to *the nation* hope of a glorious and peaceful future. One might say that the destiny of God's chosen people – the Jewish nation – was paramount in the minds and concerns of the prophets.

For three years Jesus gave his healing, his teaching and his presence to individuals. He won a following of men and women who, with various degrees of commitment, looked on him as their rabbi, their teacher or their master. But it is very unlikely that his concern was only with individuals. His Jewish upbringing must have implanted in him an awareness of God's purpose for his chosen nation and of his own calling to impart the good news of God to the nation as a whole. In this respect he must follow the example of the prophets of old: he must address the nation. And in so doing he must be prepared to suffer as the prophets of old had suffered.

In my book *The Stature of Waiting* (Darton, Longman and Todd, 1982) there is a chapter entitled 'The Road to Gethsemane'. In it I have argued that Jesus did not make his final journey to Jerusalem – to the nation's capital – *in order that* he might fulfil the purpose of God by being put to death there. I believe that he neither knew nor wished nor intended that he should be put to death. His wish and intention was to address the nation through those who had authority and power in the nation – to convey the good news of God to the nation through the leaders of the nation. He knew that his endeavour would be dangerous to himself: political and religious leaders rarely welcome new truth or new ideas, and often respond angrily and brutally to what seems to them a challenge to their authority. Jesus had no intention or wish to challenge anyone's authority: his only intention was that the nation's leaders, and through them the nation itself, should receive and welcome the good news of God which he preached.

With that intention, and for that purpose, Jesus made his journey to Jerusalem; and to help the authorities to receive and welcome his good news Jesus made his journey at a particular time of the year – the Passover season. At that season pilgrims from all over the nation would come to Jerusalem to celebrate the festival; and among them would be people from Galilee who looked to Jesus as their rabbi or teacher. Jesus would have followers, supporters, in Jerusalem at the Passover time; and he believed that he owed it to the authorities to make them aware that he was not a lone eccentric but a teacher whose good news was attractive to many and gladly received by many. The authorities could not be expected to give their attention and consideration to the words of a mere stranger from Galilee: if they were to take Jesus' words seriously they must be made aware of his 'credentials'; and those credentials were the many people who looked to him as their teacher and followed him as his supporters. For this reason, when Jesus himself came to Jerusalem, he managed that simple but public ceremony which we call the Triumphal Entry – a ceremony which would make his presence in the city known to his supporters and gather them around him – a ceremony which would make known to the authorities the enthusiasm of his followers and the strength of his support.

The so-called Triumphal Entry might be better called the Perilous Entry. What Jesus arranged to enable the authorities to take his message seriously was mistaken by the authorities for a threat to themselves and their status. The number and enthusiasm of his supporters was read as a threat to the peace of Jerusalem which the authorities in Jerusalem were required by their Roman masters to maintain. If they failed to do so they would, at best, be deprived of their office by the Roman Government or, at worst, deprived of their lives. So it came about that the Jewish authorities, fearing that Jesus' enthusiastic supporters would be a cause of disorder in the streets of Jerusalem, hastily but quietly had Jesus arrested at night on no specific charge; charged with no specific crime before the Roman Governor; and on the next day eliminated. Jesus died for being a potential trouble-maker in the busy streets of Jerusalem.

In coming to Jerusalem when he did, and entering the city as he did, Jesus risked his life – laid down his life. In demonstrating to the authorities the support which he had, he made it possible for the authorities, and through them the nation, to give serious attention to his message of good news about God. By adopting what we should call 'a high profile' in Jerusalem he gave to the authorities a motive for attending seriously to his message. One might say that he did what he did out of consideration for the point of view of the authorities and for their responsibilities as the nation's leaders: it would be irresponsible on their part to spend their time listening to an eccentric loner. But on the other hand of course there was the possibility that in his high profile Jesus would seem to the authorities to threaten the peace of Jerusalem and, as a consequence, their own status and authority.

Of this second possibility, this dark possibility, Jesus, as a realist, was well aware; and for it he prepared both his close disciples and himself. He prepared both them and himself for the worst – for his own suffering in the world and for his elimination from the world. He spoke realistically about the worst – with the realism of the brave but also with the conviction of the brave that endurance of the worst was not in vain. In the story of what we call the Passion of Jesus we see at the centre of it a very gracious, very moving and attractive figure. On his last night, within hours of his arrest, he gathers his closest disciples for a last meal together and in the course of it he asks them in the future to remember him by coming together for a simple meal. Now of course the meaning of what he said and did on that occasion has been debated and pondered by Christians for two millennia: but if we attend to the story itself we see Jesus, his life in danger, gathering his friends together to say farewell to them, laying on a meal for them, telling them how he would like to be remembered – by coming together every so often and sharing a pleasant meal together. Is not this picture of Jesus taking leave of his friends a very attractive, very gracious picture? And then, as the story of the Passion unfolds, we see at the centre of it a very calm figure, one who neither resists nor protests at what is done to him nor appeals for justice nor begs for mercy. He accepts without anger – one might even say he absorbs – the injustice of his judges, the mocking of soldiers, the taunts of his opponents, and the extremities of physical pain. He retains his dignity. When he is raised up on the cross he says little that can be heard, but in most of what is heard there is comfort for one or more of those who heard it: his words are considerate of others, gracious, welcome.

Jesus says, 'Father, forgive them, for they know not what they do.' He does not say 'I forgive you', giving the impression that he himself is in the right and those who hear him in the wrong, asserting his moral superiority to them. He prays to God to forgive them because they do not realise what they are doing. They think that they are eliminating a trouble-maker, a threat to the peace of Jerusalem: in fact they are eliminating a messenger of good news for themselves and for the whole nation. Jesus asks God to forgive them for what might be called a 'pardonable mistake'.

If, as is possible, some of the authorities who were present at Jesus' crucifixion were uneasy about what they were doing to Jesus, or became uneasy in later years, Jesus' prayer for the forgiveness of himself and his colleagues must have been very welcome, very reassuring to them. Is it not tragic beyond words that in later years so many Christians have ignored Jesus' gracious prayer as if it had never been spoken and treated Jews as, alas, they have?

Then Jesus says to the thief dying beside him, 'Verily I say unto thee, today shalt thou be with me in Paradise.' The thief asks Jesus to remember him in the future and Jesus promises him more than he asks – his presence *with* the thief in Paradise this very day. For that gracious promise the thief must, quite naturally, have been very grateful – very glad to receive it.

Jesus speaks next to his Mother and to the disciple whom he loves. To his Mother he says, 'Behold thy son' and to his disciple, 'Behold thy Mother': and thereupon the disciple takes Jesus' Mother to his own home. Their presence beside Jesus – this mark of their loyalty and love – is welcome to

Jesus but agonising to his Mother and his friend. Loyalty to him keeps them there but what they see is almost unbearable. So Jesus, in a most gracious, thoughtful way, spares them any further distress by asking each, out of loyalty to himself, to look after the other; and to look after the other means, in this agonising situation, to take the other back home. So each for the sake of the other takes the other home and neither feels disloyal to Jesus for leaving him alone: each can be glad to do for the other what Jesus has asked of her or him. Could there be a clearer expression of the thoughtfulness, the understanding, the grace of our Lord Jesus Christ than the words in which he took leave of his Mother and his friend?

The story of Jesus' crucifixion draws to a close with someone doing for him a small kindness. It is presumably one of the Roman soldiers on guard by the cross who soaks a sponge in the sharp wine which the soldiers are drinking and raises it on a stick to Jesus' lips. It is not quite clear from the story whether he does so in direct response to Jesus' cry of thirst or in response to other words of Jesus which the soldier has misheard or misunderstood; but this is not important. What is important is that as Jesus' agony draws to its close he receives and accepts a kindness from one of his executioners. He accepts what pride would reject. For one who has been wronged and mocked and ill-treated it is very difficult to accept *anything* from those at whose hands he or she has suffered – anything, that is to say, except what the sufferer himself or herself *demands* by way of apology or compensation. Our pride spurns help from those who have hurt us. Jesus did not spurn the soldier's wine.

So in this last event of Jesus life on earth we discern once again his grace. He received graciously the last kindness which was offered to him – even though it came from an enemy. I hope it is not mere sentimentality to suggest that the soldier in question remembered that incident in his later years and was glad that he had done what he did. I hope also that it is not presumptuous to suggest that when Jesus said, in the words quoted by St Paul, 'It is more blessed to give than to receive', he meant simply that it is *easier* to give than to receive. Certainly it can be very difficult to receive: it can offend our pride, challenge our self-esteem, threaten our independence. Perhaps we should say that, when we have learned to give generously, we must also learn to receive graciously. Where generous giving meets gracious receiving there occurs that situation which is called in the ancient Sanscrit language *gurtas*. That situation occurred in the last moments of Jesus' crucifixion when he received the drink which the soldier raised to his lips.

What Jesus did and said when he 'dwelt among us' in Galilee and Judaea was 'full of grace'; and when for a little while he came among us as the risen Lord his grace was still with him. I have a vivid memory of an Easter Day years ago which followed directly upon many days of bleak and cold and dismal weather. We woke on Easter morning to a different world – a world of mild air and cloudless sky and brilliant sunshine and birdsong all around us. I lived then in a cathedral city, and it so happened that on that Easter Day the morning service at the cathedral was to be broadcast to the nation. The cathedral was packed, and for a while I had to wait outside. But that was no hardship – for in the warm sunshine I stood in the cathedral garden with daffodils around my feet and cherry-blossom in its first flowering above my head; with birds racing around and singing their hearts out and from all the spires of the city the bells ringing out their Easter chimes; and, coming to me through the open doors of the cathedral, the trumpet notes of the great organ and the glorious music of the choir and the eager voices of the clergy as they preached or read from the Scriptures the great and good news for all mankind of the resurrection of Jesus Christ from the dead. Man and nature seemed to be conspiring in glorious celebration of 'Easter triumph, Easter joy'.

It was perhaps perverse of me to reflect, later on that Easter Day, that the first Easter Day had been rather different. The sun may have shone on that day, and birds sung and flowers appeared – though there is no mention of these things in the stories of the first Easter. Certainly no trumpets sounded, no bells pealed and no choirs, human or angelic, sang. When Jesus came to his disciples he came with no new radiance about his person and none of the conventional symbols of triumph and power. Now we have in the first chapter of the Book of Revelation an account by the writer of how, 'in the Spirit', he encountered the risen Jesus. It goes thus,

> I heard behind me a loud voice like a trumpet . . . Then I turned to see the voice that was speaking to me, and on turning I saw seven golden lampstands, and in the midst of the lampstands one like a son of man, clothed with a long robe and with a golden girdle round his breast: his head and his hair were white as white wool, white as snow; his eyes were like a flame of fire, his feet were like burnished bronze refined as in a furnace, and his voice was like the sound of many waters; in his right hand he held seven stars, from his mouth issued a sharp two-edged sword, and his face was like the sun shining in full strength. When I saw him I fell at his

feet as though dead. But he laid his right hand upon me,
saying, 'Fear not, I am the first and the last and the living
one; I died, and behold I am alive for evermore, and I have
the keys of death and Hades'.

This account of the appearance of the risen Christ was
probably written a generation or more after Matthew, Mark,
Luke and John had completed their work. It was written by
a visionary – a man in whom sight and imagination are
inextricably interwoven. What he sees in his mind is as vivid
as what he sees with his eyes. The risen Jesus whom he saw
in his mind was very different from the risen Jesus seen by
his disciples' eyes. They saw a figure who had passed through
death unchanged, just as he was. There was no dazzling
radiance about his figure: indeed, when first seen his figure
could be mistaken for a quite ordinary person – a gardener
or a rather ill-informed stranger on the road to Emmaus or
an unknown figure on the shore of Lake Galilee; and recognition of who he was came through marks and signs which
were his before he died – the marks of the nails driven into
him on the cross, the manner in which he blessed and broke
the bread at Emmaus. His manner with his disciples was
also unchanged by his passing through death: he who had
washed their feet on the eve of his death prepared their
breakfast on the shore of Lake Galilee. There was no tri-
umphalism in his coming back from death to his disciples:
he presented himself to them quietly, undramatically, unobtrusively; and their first response to his presence was a kind
of glad bewilderment or bewildered gladness – as Luke puts
it, 'they still disbelieved for joy'. One might say that the
presence with them, unchanged, of him who had died was
too good to be real and the report of his presence too good

to be true. One of the disciples, Thomas, was absent when Jesus was present in the upper room, and he was sceptical about what his colleagues reported. He accepted that *someone* had been present in the upper room but he would not – could not – believe that it was Jesus. He required that he himself should touch with his own hands the wounds of the crucified Jesus: only then could he believe that it was Jesus who was present.

A week later the requirement of Thomas was met: it *was* Jesus, the crucified Jesus, who was present in the upper room: it was Jesus who stood before him and showed his wounds. But what Thomas said in response was not 'Jesus!' or 'You really *are* Jesus': it was 'My Lord and my God!' It seems that during that week Thomas had been pondering on what his colleagues had told him – thinking about the implications of what they had reported to him *if* it were true. He had asked himself the question, '*If* what my colleagues say is true, who can this Jesus be? – this Jesus who was crucified and died upon the cross but is still present with us; who was derided and mocked and tortured but is still unchanged; who has endured and surmounted the extremity of suffering and survived death; who was eliminated from the world but is still among us just as he was? Who *can* he be except the ever-present One, the unchangeable One, the all-outlasting One, the everlasting One, the eternal One, God himself?' So Thomas said to the risen Jesus, 'My Lord and my God!'

No doubt other disciples of Jesus went through this same 'learning process' about the identity of Jesus and probably most of them took longer than Thomas to come to the same conclusion. The conclusion was that, in Jesus, *God* dwelt among us in the likeness of man. So the first Easter Day was not so much a triumph as an epiphany, a revelation, a disclosure. The resurrection of Jesus disclosed to the world that God, the eternal God, is 'like Jesus': it allowed and encouraged mankind to see the eternal God in Jesus and to think of the eternal God through Jesus: it justified us in saying and thinking and teaching that 'God is like Jesus'.

Since the first Easter day Christians have believed this to be so: but sometimes we are inclined to assert the converse of this belief in the words 'Jesus is like God'. In terms of logic we are justified in doing so: for if A is like B it follows that B is like A. But history does not conform to the rules of logic. History tells us that God was before Jesus dwelt among us, and that beliefs about God existed before Jesus came into the world. So to say that Jesus is like God is to believe about Jesus what was believed already about God: whereas to say that God is like Jesus is to modify or correct what was previously believed about God in the light of what we see in Jesus. The resurrection of Jesus disclosed a *new* image of God which modified or corrected what was previously believed about God.

It is upon this new image of God that the eyes of Christians must be steadily, loyally and gratefully focused. If we allow ourselves to think or say that Jesus is, or was, like God we bring into our picture of God an older image – an image in which the *grace* of our Lord Jesus Christ is marginalised or has no place at all. Our picture of God is of One who is all-powerful, just and righteous, merciful to those who seek his mercy, wrathful to those who do not, possessive and demanding of those who are his chosen people, and making with them a covenant or bargain which both sides undertake to keep. If we say that 'Jesus is like God' we tend to associate *him* with these attitudes, with these attributes in his dealings with us. We tend as Christians to see ourselves as his chosen people, his elect in an otherwise lost world; as open to his wrath when we fail to plead for his mercy, or to fulfil the terms of our covenant with him, or to meet his demands upon us; as destined on the day of our death or at his Second Coming, to stand trembling before him as a formidable Judge. In many paintings and in many church windows the figure of Jesus 'glorified' is disturbing, frightening: and so also is the music of many settings of the Requiem Mass.

In the ancient Latin hymn which we call *Te Deum* these words are addressed to the glorified Jesus: 'Thou sittest at the right hand of God in the glory of the Father: we believe that thou shalt come to be our Judge.' In the last ten words the emphasis can be put either on 'thou' or on 'Judge'. In some settings of the hymn it is put upon 'Judge' and the chord which is struck at that point is chilling: it makes the hearer shiver. In other settings the emphasis falls on 'thou' – we believe that *thou* shalt come to be our judge.' With this emphasis the words are reassuring, uplifting, good to hear, welcome. They do justice to the grace which was present among us in the works and words and ways of Jesus and which was shown by the resurrection of Jesus to be the grace of the Eternal God. The Eternal God, the One in whom we live and move and have our being, the One before whom we stand in life and in death, in time and in eternity, is *like Jesus*: he is on our side; he guides us in the exercise of our freedom but does not restrict or threaten our freedom; he is considerate of us; he does not burden us with guilt or lay down conditions on which alone he will accept us; he does not 'hold our trespasses against us'; he reconciles us to himself without humiliating us; he does not obtrude upon us his mighty and potentially terrifying powers but deals with us gently, tactfully, as parent deals with child; as friend deals with friend.

Such was the new 'image' of God which dawned upon the world in the grace of Jesus Christ and was recognised as the grace of God himself through the resurrection of Jesus Christ from the dead. The new image was very 'good news' to those who first preached and received it. It was a very attractive, very welcome image; and the natural response to it was gratitude and joy. It is sad that in the years and centuries which have followed Christians have so often, in effect, ignored or repudiated this lovely image of God and replaced it with the older image of an ever-demanding, ever-threatening, all-humiliating God. it is sad that such a good and wise man as Samuel Johnson should have lived his days in such anxiety about his relationship with God and such fear of God's judgement that the topic of death was excluded from his conversation. Millions of professing Christians have lived and died under the same dark shadow, and some still do.

St John, in the opening passage of his first letter, wrote these words: 'Truly our fellowship is with the Father and with his Son Jesus Christ. And these things write we unto you that your joy may be full. This then is the message which we have heard of him and declare unto you, that God is light and in him is *no darkness at all*.' There is no dark side to our creator: to be assured of this we need to keep close to the story of the 'things concerning Jesus' and see therein the *grace* of our Lord Jesus Christ. I believe that this closeness to the story is what St Paul had in mind when, in his letters to his converts, he so often referred to them as 'being in Christ' or 'living in Christ' or 'being brothers in Christ' and so on. Theologians have often been inclined to interpret the phrase 'in Christ' in a metaphysical or ontological sense – as if 'to be converted' is to be transformed once for all into a different person and thereby raised to a higher status in the eyes of God. I cannot believe that Paul the pastor thought in these terms. To him his converts were still fragile people, but in the good news which he had brought to them they had received an enduring, permanent, powerful resource. They were 'in Christ' in the sense that they knew the story of Jesus Christ and the power of its meaning. They knew the grace of Jesus Christ through his words and works and ways, and, through his resurrection, the grace of the Eternal God: and it was of this grace, this 'saving grace', that Paul the pastor was constantly reminding his converts.

His converts were fragile, and so are we today. Our age has been called 'the age of anxiety' and certainly we are – to quote Jesus' words to his friend Martha – 'anxious and troubled about many things'. Jesus also said that 'only one thing was needful' – that which Martha's sister Mary was doing as she sat quietly listening to Jesus' teaching about God; and certainly many of our modern forms and expressions of anxiety have their deep root in anxiety about God – does he exist or not exist? If he exists what is he like? When, if ever, can we trust God? When, if ever, should we fear him? What, if any, is God's purpose for this vast and awesome universe? In the last chapter of this book we shall look again at these questions and the anxieties which they evoke. The purpose of this chapter has been simply to draw attention to the image of God which is powerfully presented in the story of the 'things concerning Jesus': a welcome attractive, lovely image to which the natural and almost inevitable response is gratitude and joy – the image of One who 'is light', in whom there is 'no darkness at all'.

Chapter Five

THE MINISTRY OF GRACE

During that early phase in the last world war which became known as the Battle of Britain the Royal Air Force lost far too many pilots simply because they could not swim. When their aircraft was seriously damaged by enemy action the pilots, if unscathed, could come down to earth by parachute; but many came down over the English Channel and, if they could not swim, had no chance of survival. So the RAF laid down the rule that henceforth every recruit who wished to be a pilot should prove at the very beginning of his training that he could swim.

The procedure was simple but effective. Within a few days of 'signing on' in London we were transported in groups of fifty or so to Brighton and marched next morning to the Municipal Swimming Baths. At the deep end of the bath a large rubber dinghy was anchored: and the sergeant in charge of us – of whom at that stage of our training we stood in unholy dread – said peremptorily, 'You've got two minutes to get into that dinghy: go.' We went; and after two minutes about ten of us were in the dinghy and the other forty standing disconsolately on the edge or in the shallow end of the bath. (At that date there were very few swimming baths in the country at which youngsters could learn to swim.) The sergeant then addressed the disconsolates, 'You lot have got five hours to learn to swim. You'll come here for an hour every morning. If after five days you still can't swim you won't be dismissed from the RAF. Oh no, its worse than that: you'll be kept in the RAF but you'll spend the rest of the war scrubbing floors and cleaning latrines.' Those of us who were in the dinghy, including myself, listened complacently to the sergeant's threats; but then he addressed us. 'You lot,' he said, 'you've got five hours to teach this other lot to swim. I'll give you each about four pupils, and if you don't teach all of them in five days then you also will stay in the RAF – but you won't be flying – you'll be scrubbing floors and cleaning latrines till the war ends.'

He assigned the pupils to the instructors; both sides, in our innocence, were *very* strongly motivated and set to work instantly. But by the end of the session none of us was very happy. My own experience was typical. I told my pupils to keep their mouths closed; showed them the arm strokes and had them practice them in shoulder-high water; had them practice the leg strokes while holding the edge of the bath; and so on. Then I had them with their backs against the side of the bath and told them to raise one foot and kick themselves off. They did so, and sank. They tried again, and sank. They went on trying and went on sinking. I tried putting a supporting hand under the stomach of each in turn; as soon as I took it away each in turn sank. Now this propensity for sinking which my pupils showed seemed to me perverse; for if one *can* swim it is quite difficult to sink. One has to make a deliberate effort to go down: the buoyancy of the water sustains the swimmer with scarcely any effort or movement of his or her own limbs.

It was only during the second or third session that we began to realise what was going wrong: so far from being perverse our pupils were too *tense*. In their eagerness to get their bodily movements right they were stiffening, contracting their bodies and in so doing resisting or overcoming the natural buoyancy of the water. So we adopted a more casual method of teaching – racing across the bath, chasing one another into deeper water, 'messing about' in general; and this less tense, more relaxed, method worked. By the end of our five hours everyone could swim and – so far as I can remember – none of us was doomed to the inglorious future which our sergeant predicted.

In recent years I have often thought about this brief experience as a swimming-coach. The natural buoyancy of the water in a swimming bath seems to me a paradigm of the grace of God. It is all around us; it sustains us. But we can resist it – and this resistance may or may not be deliberate. A swimmer *can*, if he or she wishes, sink to the bottom of the swimming bath – can overcome the natural buoyancy of water; but a non-swimmer does so unintentionally, by no wish of his or her own. Swimmers insulate themselves deliberately from the buoyancy of water; non-swimmers insulate themselves inadvertently by their intense preoccupation with 'doing the right thing' – with making the right movements of arms and legs.

So we may insulate ourselves from the sustenance – the buoyancy – of the grace of God by preoccupation with our own performance in the world, by – so to speak – taking ourselves too seriously. We may fail to recognise 'the grace of God which has dawned upon the world' because our eyes, so far from scanning the horizon, are introverted – looking into ourselves. What we see within ourselves is of infinite variety: some of us, at certain times, are deeply concerned with our ambitions and prospects in our careers; some with our home life and the future of our children; some with our bank accounts or our social status or what other people think of us; some with our health or our declining faculties; some with our duties in the world and some with the unfairness of the world to us; some with our talents and some with our defects. So one could go on: our deep concerns and preoccupations are endless. Some, no doubt, are more worthy than others, but the outcome of all alike is transient. It has been said that time is 'a perpetual perishing': it has also been said that time is 'a great healer': and both statements are true. The new car which was once the object of our ambition, and for which we yearned and saved, becomes in time an 'old banger' of which we are ashamed; and the children who once worried us by their behaviour become in time our pride and joy. The concerns with which we were once preoccupied and even obsessed cease to be concerns; but in the course of time they give place to other concerns. Particular things and situations which give us 'cause for concern', 'cause to worry', come and go; but the *disposition* to be concerned, to worry about *something* seems to be innate in us. It seems as if we are born with a 'hole in the mind' waiting for occupation by anxiety and worry over our own performance in the world.

St Augustine identified this 'hole' in his words, 'O God, Thou has made us for Thyself and our heart is restless till it rest in Thee.' His words echo the words of Jesus when he said, 'Martha, Martha, you are anxious and troubled with many things: *one* thing is needful.' The 'hole in the mind' *needs* to be filled with awareness of God, attention to God, peace with God: and if it is not so filled it will be occupied by anxiety and worry. But of course it is not enough that the hole should be filled by attention to 'some kind of God'. We speak of misers as 'making money their god' and I imagine that few people are more anxious and prone to worry than misers. And much the same is true of people who make a god out of drugs or any other form of addiction. We can rest only in the God who has made us, in whom 'we live and move and have our being', in him who has been disclosed to us in and through the words and works and ways of Jesus Christ and, decisively and unambiguously, by his resurrection from the dead. We can rest only when the eyes of our mind are focused on that image of God which was presented to the world in the grace of our Lord Jesus Christ.

As Christians we are inheritors and beneficiaries of that image. It enables us to live in 'the peace of God which passes all understanding'. It empowers us to put our trust in God without fear or apprehension or anxiety. Our knowledge of the grace of God naturally evokes gratitude and joy in us: *charis* naturally responds to *charis*. And *charis* in us naturally evokes *charis* in others. Joyful gratitude cannot 'keep itself to itself': it is naturally attractive and expansive. And so as Christians we are not only beneficiaries of our knowledge of the grace of God which 'has dawned upon the world' in Jesus Christ: we are also called, and even driven, to impart to others that knowledge, that 'good news', which we have ourselves received.

No Christian has been more compulsively driven to share the good news with others than St Paul. In one of his letters to his Corinthian converts he wrote: 'God was in Christ reconciling the world to himself, not holding their trespasses against them and giving to us the message of reconciliation.' The story of Jesus which Paul himself and other evangelists told in the market-places of the world was the *message* of God being reconciled to us and we to him; and now that message is entrusted to 'us' – put into our hands to be passed on to 'them' whose trespasses God 'does not hold against them' – that is to say, to all the people in the world who have not yet heard the message. In the same passage in his letter Paul also wrote that 'in Christ God was reconciling us to himself and giving to us the *ministry* of reconciliation'.

It is significant that he used in one passage the two different phrases 'the message of reconciliation' and 'the ministry of reconciliation'. His reason for doing so probably lay in his own experience as a Christian: at first he believed himself called to be simply a messenger of reconciliation, but later he found himself called to be a *minister* of reconciliation to and among his converts who had already received the message. As they kept in touch with him and he with them he realised that they 'had problems'. Though they had all received the message of reconciliation things were not going altogether smoothly among them – there were differences and scandals and misunderstandings among them; and Paul, though now far away from them, could not wash his hands of them, could not be content to say 'it's nothing to do with me now'. So he took on the task of writing to them long letters of encouragement and correction and guidance and rebuke and explanation and so on. It is remarkable, when one thinks of it, that Paul – constantly travelling from place to place, constantly meeting new people, troubled by illness and poor eyesight, frequently put in custody, several times flogged or 'beaten with rods' – should have found the time and summoned up the energy to write these long and powerful letters which are now our treasure. As he wrote or dictated them he must have realised that Christians have a responsibility which goes beyond that of delivering the message of reconciliation: and he called this further responsibility the ministry of reconciliation.

———

Now let us consider this twofold responsibility as it applies to us in the world of today. Let us take first our responsibility for the message of reconciliation. One of my earliest memories at the church in which I was brought up was of occasional visits from men and women who had gone out from their homes to be missionaries overseas in Africa and India and Japan and elsewhere and had returned home briefly on furlough. They told us stories of their work overseas. I remember in particular a priest-missionary telling of an occasion when there came to his church one Easter Day a group of people who were strangers to him and who knew nothing of Jesus. He told us of their earnest attention as he told them the story of Jesus and of their joy and enthusiasm when the story came to its denouement on the first Easter Day. What the priest told us made a deep impression on a boy of my age: but that was over sixty years ago. In the intervening years the world has greatly changed and my childhood vision of the Christian missionary as a heroic figure venturing to the ends of the earth – 'to heathen lands afar' – to tell to the ignorant the good news of Jesus has become out of date. To say this is not to disparage the motives of the Christians of the past who went out as overseas missionaries or to belittle their heroism or their achievements: but as the world becomes ever smaller, ever closer to being one world, it becomes ever more important that we should respect the cultures of others, the histories and sensitivities of others, the traditions of others. Christians still have a Gospel to proclaim – good news to tell to *all mankind*: but that news cannot be welcome if the manner of its proclamation smacks of condescension, racial or intellectual superiority or lack of respect for the hearers' culture and traditions. My romantic boyhood vision of the heroic overseas missionary penetrating courageously the darkness of heathen lands afar, riding roughshod over the customs and prejudices of his ignorant and uncivilised hearers and dragging them triumphantly from darkness into light was, no doubt, already out of date when I harboured it: it is certainly out of date now. The call of Christians to be overseas messengers of God's reconciliation must surely be limited to men and women who are already familiar with the land to which they go as missionaries, feel themselves at home there, are already at ease with the people of the land and already respectful of their culture and traditions.

It is not overseas but in our own country that the need for messengers of reconciliation is most evident. I have in mind the important matter of Christian education. One often hears from advocates or supporters of Christian education the argument that 'the children of today are the church of tomorrow' – an argument which implies that Christian education is a kind of investment from which dividends will be received by the Christian community in the future. This argument sounds 'commercial' and is certainly inadequate. To tell to a child the story of Jesus is to implant in that child a seed which in due time may become a source of healing in the crises and distresses of adult life: it is to impart to a child a precious resource which adult Christians treasure. To deny this resource to a child is to deprive that child of a gift and blessing which adult Christians, as messengers of reconciliation, *owe* to him or her: and a child to whom this resource is denied is as truly 'deprived' as a child who never gets enough to eat. Now of course there are *difficulties* in the world of today in telling the story of Jesus to children. Children love stories, but in the age of television they are exposed to a plethora of stories competing for their attention – exciting stories, vividly presented, appealing to their eyes as well as to their ears. Children over-exposed to television have little attention to spare for the story of Jesus. So parents and teachers who are responsible for telling children that story have a very difficult task. It is probably impossible unless the story is told 'in the right atmosphere' – unless there is the right relationship between the parent or teacher on the one side and the child on the other. Children are more sensitive than adults to *who it is* that tells a story: a story *means more* to a child if it is told by 'mum' or 'dad' than if it is told by a stranger; if it is told by a teacher whom one really likes than if it is told by one whom one 'hates'. The calling of Christian parents and teachers to make known to the new generation the saving story of Jesus is *very* demanding nowadays: those who undertake it seriously are worthy of the greatest respect and admiration from their fellow Christians, and all Christians must face the fact that many children in our land know nothing of Jesus (except that 'Jesus' is a familiar swear-word) – not because they are Muslims or Hindus or Sikhs but because they are children whom we have left deprived.

It follows from this that an increasing number of young adults in our country are in need of the *message* of reconciliation. How can such people be reached by the message? Evangelists like St Paul simply travelled – though their travelling was rarely simple – to the news-hungry market-places of the world, raised their voices, drew a crowd and gave their message – told succinctly the story of Jesus. John Wesley's method of evangelism was much the same as Paul's – travelling thousands of miles a year on horseback, preaching 40,000 sermons, gathering huge crowds, mainly of poor people working in the new industrial towns of our country.

But the evangelistic method of Paul and Wesley is hardly practicable or even conceivable today. Quite apart from the fact that both men were inspired with extraordinary energy, the change in the world during the two hundred years between Wesley's time and ours has been vastly greater than was the change during the seventeen centuries which separated Wesley from Paul. What might be called 'street-corner evangelism' is bound to be ineffective in a society which, so far from being hungry for news, is over-fed and even choked by the news disseminated by the public voices of the media; and those few brave but unrealistic evangelists who raise their voices on Tower Hill or elsewhere tend to attract their meagre audiences out of, at the best, passing curiosity and, at the worst, the desire of hecklers to get a laugh. The well-known evangelists of the world today – household names, especially in America – go indoors to broadcast their message on radio or television or, by their reputation, to fill a hall with admirers to whom their message is already known. They rarely meet and reach personally people to whom the message of reconciliation is unknown. Furthermore, some of the people who are known as evangelists are not 'messengers-of-good-news' at all: what they tell is predominantly bad news – threatening, alarming news. An American friend of mine who is very familiar with the message of such 'evangelists' gave me this analogy. The manager of an hotel comes into the restaurant at dinner time and says 'Ladies and gentlemen, I have good news for you. The hotel is on fire. The flames are spreading. The exits are ablaze. The fire brigade is on strike. Death by burning is extremely painful. So I am sure you would like to know that as manager I have a private exit which is untouched and through which I can take you all. I'm sure too that you would like to leave a donation for making use of my exit.' Such, said my friend, is the kind of 'good news' which is often to be heard from certain radio and television stations which claim to be Christian. Even in St Paul's day there were in Galatia men who were 'perverting the gospel of Christ' and Paul was at his most passionate in his condemnation of them and his warning to his converts to have no truck with them.

So how is one to reach men and women who were deprived in childhood of the message of reconciliation, who know nothing of the story of Jesus? Many of them were also deprived in other ways in their childhood and have in consequence problems or handicaps more severe than the generality of us. It is not to be expected that a person so burdened will pay attention, and respond positively, to the message of a stranger – however loudly and passionately the stranger speaks. There is a possibility of winning thoughtful attention and a positive response only if there is the right personal relationship between the speaker and the hearer; and this right relationship might be defined as that of mutual understanding and affection and respect. I have heard several prison chaplains make this point. Thundering appeals in the prison chapel to 'give yourself to the Lord Jesus' are of little avail: what is necessary is private conversation between chaplain and prisoner – conversation in which each grows in understanding of the other's point of view, in considerateness for it, in mutual trust, in the wish of each to do small acts of kindness to the other. And of course what is true of the work of prison chaplains is also true of thousands of Christians who are called to be social workers. Probably their contract of employment forbids them to be explicit messengers to their clients of what Christians believe or, indeed, of what is believed in any other religion: but as

Christians they are called to enact in their relationships with their clients the *grace* of Jesus Christ – his considerateness for others, his patience, his availability to all, his tact, his manner of forgiveness, his courage. It is by what they *are* in their profession, in their personal and private and face-to-face encounters with their clients, that they can be messengers of reconciliation.

We have been considering how we can, and how we cannot, deliver the message of reconciliation in the world of today. Let us now consider the ministry of reconciliation which is also given and entrusted to us. As we have seen, Paul made this distinction between the two because his own life 'in Christ' had gone through two distinct phases. Having won converts in many cities by the message he brought to them, and having heard how their community was now faring, he felt himself called to do what he could to *keep them together* as a community – to undertake through his letters a ministry of reconciliation. The Greek word translated as 'ministry' is *diaconia*, and it had at the time no specifically religious or political connotation. *Diaconia* meant simply the 'service' which is done by, or expected from, a servant or a slave – the service which is *needed* by a person or community; and what was most needed by some of Paul's converts – especially his troublesome converts in Corinth – was unity in Christ among themselves. Although they had all received the same good news and committed themselves by the same baptism to the same faith in Christ, their new outlook on life did not in itself provide instant solutions for all problems or instant answers to all questions. Practical problems and down to earth questions were still evoking differences among Christians. Among the Corinthians there were, for instance, differences about food – about what a

Christian should or should not eat. Some of Paul's converts were Jews, of whom some thought themselves still bound by the Mosaic Law concerning what one might eat and how it must be prepared, while others, including Paul himself, thought themselves free from the Mosaic regulations. Other converts were Gentiles and had been brought up in religions which offered up animal sacrifices to various idols. It appears that some of the meat, having been offered to idols, was afterwards put up for sale in the market-place – whether legally or by underhand dealing we do not know. So for Gentiles the problem arose whether as Christians they should eat meat which, having been as it were, 'spiritually contaminated' by its association with idol-worship, was now on sale on a market stall. And it was not only over matters of food that the Corinthains had differences. Problems arose also over marriage and sexual matters in general – should a Christian who was not yet married abstain from marriage? Should a Christian whose wife or husband was not a Christian divorce or otherwise part company with his or her partner? Should a widow feel free to marry again or should she remain a widow? Should a Christian abstain altogether from sexual intercourse? And more problems and differences arose over the status of slaves who became Christians: should they think of themselves as no longer slaves to their masters or should they refuse a master's offer to make them freedmen?

With such various problems Paul the pastor wrestled for the sake of his converts. This was the ministry – the 'service' – which he gave to them in and through his letters. He did not lay down the law to them; he did not write to them as one who knows all the answers: he *wrestled* with the problems. He did so with the message of reconciliation always the back-cloth against which he saw the practical problems of his converts. He was constantly reminding them of the message – constantly referring to it not as solving the practical problems for them but as putting their problems into the right proportions. The message which his converts had received and accepted was, so to speak, their charter of a new freedom – freedom for Jewish converts from the Law of Moses and its restrictions, freedom for Gentile converts from their anxieties and superstitions, freedom 'in Christ' which in the purpose of God is to be extended to all mankind. Paul, in his dramatic encounter on the road to Damascus, had received that charter; in his work as an evangelist he had imparted it to others; and now in later years he was called *to keep together* his converts in various cities – to unite them in communities so strong and mutually loyal within themselves that they would naturally attract new members and become ever-expanding communities until the message of reconciliation was known to all mankind and the purpose of God fulfilled. To quote the final sentence of his advice to Corinthians who were unmarried. 'I say this for your own benefit, not to put any restrictions upon you but to promote good order and to secure your *undivided* devotion to the Lord.'

The purpose of his ministry to his converts was that they should become and remain communities 'full of grace' – that is to say *attractive* communities, communities welcome in the cities and naturally drawing to themselves new converts, new members – gracious communities to which the city as a whole would respond with gratitude and joy. In his ministry to his converts Paul constantly emphasised the need for mutual *considerateness* within the Christian community – for mutual respect for the point of view of others, for mutual understanding of the upbringing of others and of their

present situation. In wrestling with the problems of his converts he recognised the new freedom which Christians had
received in and through Christ: he accepted the cliché 'all
things are lawful'. But he added to the cliché the qualification
'but not all things are helpful: not all things build up. Let
no one seek his own good but the good of his neighbour.'
He accepted that Christians are free to eat whatever meat is
offered by the host at a dinner table – whether or not it
is forbidden by the Law of Moses, whether or not is has
been offered to idols. But he added the rider, 'if someone
says to you "This has been offered in sacrifice", then out
of consideration for the man who informed you, and, for
conscience sake – I mean his conscience not yours – do not
eat it.' He recognised that the rider was, on the face of it,
unfair – 'for why should my liberty be determined by another
man's scruples?' But he adhered in general to the view that
Christians should be very sensitive to those whom he called,
tactfully, 'weaker brethren'. Christians must not, in the exercise of their freedom, shock weaker brethren or put stumbling
blocks in their way or despise or ignore their scruples or
affront their conscience. If more sophisticated Christians do
so they 'destroy this weak brother for whom Christ died'.
There was one Christian in Corinth who was *flaunting* his
freedom by cohabiting with his father's wife; and, what is
more, some of his colleagues were rather proud to have
among them a member so boldly and brazenly immoral.
Both the man and his colleagues received a tremendous
rebuke from Paul and the solemn demand that the man be
instantly expelled from the Christian community. Freedom
flaunted was, to Paul, freedom abused: and the abuse of
freedom would impair the unity of the Christian community.
He likened the behaviour of the brazenly immoral man to

'leaven which spreads through the whole lump' – to what we should call the cancerous growth spreading through the whole body. The image of the Christian community as 'the body of Christ' was, of course, prominent in Paul's teaching: each Christian was a functioning member of the body, each both dependent on and contributing to the well-being of the body as a whole, and the grossly immoral man must be expelled from the body lest he impair the functioning of the body as a whole.

Having dealt in his letter with this particular and distressing case, Paul went on to write in more general terms about the relationship between the Christian community and 'immoral' people. He referred back to a previous letter – he must have written at least three letters to his troublesome Corinthians – in which he had advised them not to associate with immoral people (the Greek word has a specific sexual connotation) or with greedy people or robbers or idol-worshippers. Now he wished to correct this. He did not mean that they should dissociate themselves from such people who were outside the Christian community – to do so would be to isolate themselves 'from the world': he meant that they should dissociate themselves from such people who were within the community – 'their brothers'. He did not say that such people should be expelled from the community, but that they should be cold shouldered, made aware that their behaviour was inappropriate, criticised for it. As for immoral or greedy people or robbers or idolaters *outside* the community, they were not for Christians to criticise or judge – God would be their judge.

There are two points to be noticed in this particular passage in Paul's letter. He did not think that the notoriously immoral man who was to be expelled from the community was thereby 'damned to all eternity'. On the contrary, he wrote 'you are to deliver this man to Satan for the destruction of the flesh that his spirit may be saved in the day of the Lord Jesus.' What he meant by 'delivering him to Satan for the destruction of the flesh' is not clear, but, in the light of Paul's association of Satan with sin and of sin with death, I would suggest that 'delivering him to Satan' meant 'praying for his early death' in order that, before he sinned yet more, his spirit might be saved in the day of the Lord Jesus. When the Christians of Corinth gathered formally, with Paul's own authority behind them, to expel this man from the community they were to pray that his sinful flesh might soon be destroyed and his spirit saved in and through the Lord Jesus. Even the most notorious of sinners are not beyond the saving power and will of the Lord Jesus.

The second point is this. Paul did not believe that it was the calling of the Christian community to isolate itself from the world outside it or to criticise or pass judgement on or condemn that world. Neither as messenger nor as minister of reconciliation did he do so. Both in his preaching and in his writing he told or reminded people of 'good news for all mankind' and of the 'fruits of the Spirit' which the good news had implanted in them – 'love, joy, peace, patience, kindness, goodness, faithfulness, gentleness, self-control'; and he contrasted these welcome 'fruits' with the 'works of the flesh' – 'fornication, impurity, licentiousness, idolatry, sorcery, enmity, strife, jealousy, anger, selfishness, dissention, party spirit, envy, drunkenness, carousing and the like'. He warned his converts in Galatia that those who do the works of the flesh 'shall not inherit the kingdom of God'. But he did not say or imply that the fruits of the Spirit appeared only in the Christian community or that the works of the flesh were to be found only in the world outside it. Paul knew the truth which St John in his gospel expressed in the words 'Christ came into the world not to condemn the world but that the world through him should be saved.' Paul's calling was not to convict and convince the world of its wickedness but to win the world into acceptance of the good news of God and to sustain the world as one enduring community of love, joy, peace and all the other fruits of the Spirit. No one can be won into membership of such a community by criticism, condemnation, blame or threats.

Paul's ministry to his converts was 'full of grace'. By his letters he kept in touch with them: in Dr Johnson's phrase, 'he kept his friendship with them in good repair' – at what a cost of time and energy who can tell? As we read them today we are struck by Paul's affection for his converts, the number of friends whom he remembers by name, the warmth of his congratulations on all that is going well in the community, the thoroughness and earnestness with which he wrestles with their problems and differences. His converts in the important city of Corinth seem to have included an 'intellectual' element and, perhaps for this reason, were more troublesome than most; but in his letters Paul does not ignore this element. In the two most famous chapters of his first letter to the Corinthians – the thirteenth and the fifteenth – he wrote words most carefully chosen and most reasoned in their argument. His description of the love which transcends all other human gifts and virtues, his analysis of love, is still recognised as 'a thing of beauty', 'a joy for ever'; and his argument with certain Christians who were asserting that 'there is no such thing as the resurrection of the dead' is so elegantly expressed and so decisively reasoned that it remains convincing to the most argumentative of Christian intellectuals today. Although Paul had many occasions to correct or rebuke his converts, he never ceased to write to them as their friend and to be considerate of their point of view.

This is particularly evident in two other letters which Paul wrote to his converts. His converts in Philippi were by no means so troublesome as those in Corinth, and his letter to them was intimate, affectionate and wholly encouraging. Paul wrote from prison – probably in Rome and probably in his final imprisonment from which he went to his death. The generous Philippians had sent one of their number – a man called Epaphroditus – to bring gifts to the prisoner. It seems that Epaphroditus had fallen ill when he reached his destination, and nearly died during his illness. Now he was fit to return home, and Paul sent with him his letter of thanks to the Christians of Philippi. It is a lovely letter. Paul was naturally grateful both for the gift itself and for 'the thought behind it': but he did not wish to exploit the generosity of the Philippians by giving the impression that he was in desperate need of their gifts. He had to say 'Thank you' without, in effect, asking for more, and also without depreciating or belittling the worth to him of what the kindly Philippians had already sent. He had to be what we call today 'tactful' in his letter: and when we read the letter today we can almost see the writer choosing the exact words in which to express his gratitude to his friends without exploiting their kindness.

The other particularly tactful letter which Paul wrote is the shortest of his letters which have survived. It was also written from prison and was addressed to Philemon, a convert of Paul, in whose house – we know not where – the local community of Christians gathered. A slave belonging to Philemon had run away from him – a slave to whom his master had given the name 'Onesimus', which means 'helpful', and who, therefore, was presumably valuable to his master. At that period, of course, Roman Law gave to slave-owners unlimited rights and powers over their slaves, and a slave who ran away from his master might expect, if he were recaptured, brutal punishment or even death. Onesimus, having run away, somehow came into touch with Paul when he was in prison, was converted by Paul and became his valued and beloved servant in the prison. Now Onesimus was to return to his master – whether by his own decision or by Paul's persuasion we do not know – and take with him Paul's letter to Philemon. In it Paul recognises Philemon's legal right to do what he wills with Onesimus; hints that Philemon may have lost money through the absence of his slave and undertakes to repay what he has lost; gently and affectionately reminds Philemon that he owes something to Paul for converting him; appeals to him to receive Onesimus back no longer as just a slave but as a 'brother in Christ'; ends with thanks for Philemon's prayers for him in his imprisonment and his hopes that some day he may be able to come and stay with Philemon in his own house.

Philemon must have responded positively to Paul's appeal: he must have *treasured* the letter – otherwise it would not have survived for two thousand years. For us it is a classic example of how Paul performed his ministry of reconcili-ation. He took account of Philemon's point of view: no doubt in that age the loss of a slave was as maddening to the owner as the theft of one's car is in our age, and Paul made allow-ances for Philemon's feelings about the situation. He wrote as one who was on the side of *both* Onesimus *and* Phile-mon; as one who was the friend of both and, of each, 'the brother in Christ'. He did not lay down or discuss with Philemon the general principle that 'slavery is unacceptable' or that Roman Law about the master–slave relationship is 'unjust'. He dealt – tactfully, effectively, 'healingly' – with one particular situation. One is reminded of William Blake's words, 'He who would do good must do it by minute particulars.' Paul would not have dissented from these succinct and perceptive words. As a minister of reconciliation he found himself called to be, in his own words, 'all things to all men' and he accepted his calling. In modern parlance the phrase 'all things to all men'; has become derogatory – it suggests a person who is fickle or obsequious to others or unprincipled; but for Paul it had no such connotation. It meant for him that he was called to be aware of the *variety* of people within each Christian community; to be sensitive to their various backgrounds and gifts and at the same time to hold them together as a united community, attractive to others and worthy to be called the body of Christ; to be particularly considerate of weaker brethren and lean over backwards to give them no offence and set no stumbling block in their way; to take seriously the questions which were asked in the community and the problems which arose; and to do all this, and to be all this, against the majestic background of the message of reconciliation which all have, through Christ and in Christ, received and believed. To his beloved Philippians Paul wrote 'I can do all things through him who strengthens me', and we should think of him not as 'all things to all men' but as 'a man in Christ', 'a man for all seasons'. There was *grace* in his ministry: there was in his ministry that quality which attracts and appeals to people, which draws people into a community and holds them together as a united and enduring community which will naturally grow and expand.

First and foremost in his life as a Christian came – as he confided to his friends in Philippi – 'the excellence of the knowledge of Christ Jesus my Lord', by comparison with which he counted all other things as mere 'refuse' or 'dung'. And then, later, he accepted the ministry of – as he wrote to the Corinthians – 'promoting good order' among converts who had already received 'the excellence' of that knowledge in the message of reconciliation. When he wrote to the Corinthians that 'all things should be done decently and in order' he had in mind much more than the *worship* of the Christian community; he had in mind all that holds together and sustains that community – mutual respect and understanding and consideration and tactfulness. By the grace of his own ministry of reconciliation he implanted and sustained grace in each community of converts: grace evoked the response of grace, *charis* met *charis*.

Now let us begin to consider what the ministry of reconciliation requires of *us* – of Christians in the vastly different world of today. Let us start with two very obvious and relevant differences. The first is that the boundary of 'the Christian community' is far less clear today than it was in the years when Paul was writing his letters: the second is that the word 'ministry' tends to suggest today a calling which is confined to a certain number of Christians and withheld from the majority: in Paul's time this distinction within the community as a whole had not yet been formally recognised.

The infant church to which Paul ministered consisted of small groups of people who, having heard and assented to the message of reconciliation, were baptised 'into Christ' and came together regularly in the house of one of their number. They called themselves Christians – 'Christ's people' – and their community 'the body of Christ'; and the boundary of their community was as clearly defined as that of, say, the British Legion or the Golf Club in a small town of today. But who would be bold enough to define what is meant when a person is called a Christian in the world of today? The new edition of the *Oxford English Dictionary* offers four possibilities: 'a person who has received Christian baptism', 'an adherent of Christ's teaching', 'a person exhibiting Christian qualities' and, colloquially, a person who is 'kind, fair, decent'. I recall the funeral of a man who was a self-confessed and voluble atheist. His family were not of that mind and arranged that his funeral service should take place in the local church. The vicar, knowing the situation, began his homily with the words, 'A. B. was not a Christian', and then went on to speak, with respect and appreciation, of A. B.'s honesty, of his care for his family, of his pleasant personality, of his patience in his last illness and so on. But unfortunately the members of A. B.'s family were so shocked by the vicar's opening words that they could not 'hear' the appreciative words which followed and took great offence at the 'insult' to the old man. In the language of today it is risky to say of someone that he or she is 'a Christian' or 'a real Christian' – for this might imply a slur on 'certain-people-whom-I-have-in-mind-but-will-not-mention'; and it is more risky still to say that someone is *not* a Christian. The boundary of the Christian community is no longer definable in the 'one world' in which we live: no computer can inform us of the number of Christians who inhabit the world or of their distribution in various states and continents.

But our inability to define and identify our 'fellow Christians' in the world of today is not as serious as it may sound. For we believe that Christ died and rose again from death for the sake of *all* mankind – that the 'good news', the message of God's reconciliation, is good news for *all* mankind. Whether or not a certain person believes the news is, in a sense, immaterial: for the good news itself remains intact, it is still *true*. As William Blake wrote,

> Mock on, mock on, Voltaire, Rousseau:
> Mock on, mock on: 'tis all in vain!
> You throw the sand against the wind,
> And the wind blows it back again.

Whatever a person may believe or disbelieve, God remains what Jesus showed him to be, and that person's destiny remains in the kind hands of him whom Jesus has disclosed to us. Whatever a person may think or believe or imagine about his or her own destiny, in time or in eternity, that person is not *lost*: he or she is embraced for ever in the everlasting arms of him who came and dwelt among us in the human form of Jesus Christ. Therefore it is immaterial in the last analysis whether a particular person identifies himself or herself as an atheist or a Christian or a Jew or a Muslim or an unbeliever. To quote the last stanza of one of those wonderful poems which Dietrich Bonhoeffer wrote in his prison cell shortly before his execution in 1945:

> God goeth to every man when sore bestead,
> Feedeth body and spirit with his bread
> For Christians, heathens alike He hangeth dead:
> And both alike forgiving.

When we go about our Christian duty or calling of telling the story of Jesus to our children or to adults who have not yet heard it our motive is not to save them from being lost, rejected by God, damned: it is to enable them to live their lives unafraid of God, unthreatened by God, free from anxiety about God, seeing through Jesus what God is really like, turning to him in their troubles, glad and grateful to have such a good friend in whom they can trust. I cannot help recalling at this point a boy who was *not* so enabled. His mother, a single parent and a stranger to me, came to ask advice about her son who, in his middle teens, was getting into quite serious trouble with the police. I did not know the boy and had to ask whether he had had any contact with religious teaching in his upbringing – at school or a church or a youth club or anywhere else. The mother did not seem to know. 'But', she said, 'he gets that at home: I teach him myself about God.' I asked her, rather tentatively, *what* she taught him about God. 'Oh', she immediately answered, 'I teach him that if he does wrong God will punish him.' I said, even more tentatively, 'Do you ever teach him that when he does wrong God will forgive him?' 'No', she said scornfully, and left the house in a considerable huff at my suggestion. What chance had her son of thinking of God as his friend? He is probably deprived for life of the joy and peace of knowing God as Jesus showed him to be; but this of course does not mean that he is a 'lost soul', doomed and damned by God for all eternity.

So it is that, in a particular town or parish, we do not need to define the boundary between Christians and those who profess some other faith or no faith at all. Our Father in heaven is Father of each and all who reside in the vicinity, and each is our sister or our brother. Each is entitled to equal courtesy and consideration and respect: we owe to each sensitivity to his or her point of view. We are to be 'good neighbours' to those who live around us, whatever may be their race or colour or religion. We are not to ostracise people whose religious practices are different from our own, and on the other hand we are not to attempt to undermine their faith in those practices and so alienate them from their family and from the religious community to which they belong. But of course in virtually every town and parish in this country there are many people who are uncertain of where they stand in matters of religion. They do not associate themselves with Judaism or Islam or Hinduism or any of the great religions other than Christianity, but their attachment to Christianity is uncertain, hesitant, loose, insecure. They would be inclined to say, 'I am a Christian, but I don't go to church' or, conversely, 'I don't go to church, but I am a Christian'. It is the Church rather than 'what the Church believes' which tends to put a stumbling block in the path of such people and make their attachment to Christian belief hesitant and insecure. They feel that they would be ill at ease in attending a church or fear that they would be out of place there or are anxious lest they should expose themselves to embarrassment or to commitment beyond their will or capacity. The regular public worship of God, which for many of us is a duty and a joy, is *very difficult* for others – even for others whose faith in God through Christ is no less sincere and firm than our own. Two particular incidents which illustrate this stick in my mind.

In my salad days as a curate the church organist asked me to visit an old man, a near neighbour of his, who was near to death. I said that I would, and the organist added, considerately, 'I think I ought to warn you. You may get a bad reception. Mr So-and-so has never had any time for the church – I think he's an atheist, and he may be rude to you or turn you away.' I thanked him for the warning and went to the house. The front door opened directly onto the pavement, and it was not locked; so I stepped directly into the room where the old man lay. It was a dreary afternoon, and the old man raised himself a little in bed to peer and see who his visitor was. We had never seen each other before, and it must have been by my clerical collar that he recognised *what* I was. For he smiled at me and took my hand and would not let it go: and he said, 'Thank you for coming ... I've said my prayers every day of my life ... Thank you.' Even the old man's near neighbour did not know his private, lifelong faith and trust in God.

The second incident was in a hospital ward. I was on my way to visit a parishioner when the ward sister asked me to go first to a patient who was lying in a curtained bed in the corner. 'I was just going to attend to him,' she said, 'but he has asked to see a clergyman; so perhaps you will go to him first.' I went behind the curtains and found a man who was having a blood-transfusion and haemorrhaging at the same time. There was much dried blood around his mouth and on his face and hands and he found it difficult to speak; but he managed to say, 'Padré, will you be coming here again tonight?' I said that I would, and he asked me to bring a couple of cans of beer for him when I came. When I came with the beer a doctor was in the ward, and I asked him if it was all right for the patient to have the beer. 'Oh yes', he said sadly, 'it doesn't matter much what he has now.' The patient took the beer and was refreshed and able to speak more easily. He told me that he was a prison-warder, aged 44, happily married and the father of two young sons. Six months before he had been told that he was suffering from leukaemia and could expect to live no more than six months: and now the six months were up. 'I think I'm dying, Padré,' he said. 'Of course I'm still fighting for my life – for my wife's sake and the kids' sake: but I don't think I'll win. And what I wanted to tell you, Padré – the reason I asked for the beer – is this. I've never been what *you* would call religious, Padré – the wife is more inclined that way: but I believe in God and what I want you to know, Padré, is that in the last few days – five days to be exact – I've found the peace of God. It grows on me day by day, Padré: I can't tell you how wonderful it is.' Then we shook hands, and he smiled and said, 'Take that bit of good cheer home with you, will you, Padré.' He died later in the night. I never knew his name: but it seems right that people other than myself should share that 'bit of good cheer' – his dying testimony to the peace of God.

In virtually every town and parish in this country there is at least one church. In it will be found at regular intervals much the same group of people: and, to a greater or lesser degree, they will feel a loyalty to their church and a responsibility for its well-being. They can sing truthfully, 'We love the place, O God, wherein thine honour dwells' and many can add, equally truthfully, 'The joy of thine abode all earthly joy excels'. They come together to share in the public worship of the God whose grace is disclosed to mankind in the story of Jesus Christ; and in their worship, however formal or informal, there is, in word and sacrament, constant reference to that story – to that 'good news', to the message of God's reconciliation to and with all mankind through Jesus Christ our Lord. In the worship of their church people keep close to the story of Jesus; they are reminded of it; it is brought to the forefront of the mind, and in its light other things are seen in their true proportions. In its light – to quote Mother Julian – 'all is well: all is *very* well.' The public worship of the church is both a reminder that, in the last analysis, 'all is well' and an expression of joy and gratitude that 'all is well'; and there are many churches in which, whether the worshippers are few or many, the act of worship is both an effective reminder of the story of Jesus and a worthy expression of gratitude and joy.

But of course in every town and parish a great deal more is happening than the worship which goes on in the church. Beneath the surface, behind the doors, of even the most peaceful village or the most attractive country town things are happening which are of great importance in the private lives of people and families – things over which particular people lie awake at night in their distress or delight. It is not over general issues that we 'lose our sleep' – the state of the nation, the statistics of crime, the rise or fall in the bank rate, the opinion polls published in the newspapers: it is by 'minute particulars' that we are most deeply distressed or delighted. These particularities are *existentially* powerful: they reach not only to our thoughts but also to the deeper level of our feelings. So it is that, beneath the surface, the most placid of towns or villages is *seething* with activity: someone has had a row with a neighbour and feels very angry; someone has made it up with a neighbour and feels much relieved; someone living alone feels lonely and unwanted, and someone else feels delighted by a visit or a letter; someone has lost his or her job and is very anxious about the future, and someone has found a job and feels 'over the moon'; some parents delight in every minute with their little children and some whose children are older find themselves very worried by their behaviour. Most people at some time experience illness and pain and, later on, the pleasure of being much better and the relief of their pain; some people feel themselves successful in most of the things that they do and others feel themselves consistent failures; all people feel sad when those who are dear to them suffer or die.

So one could go on. All of us are subject to the powerful impact of moods and feelings – whether we live in a peaceful village or in an inner city in which homelessness and noise and crime abound. In both alike things are happening which *matter* to particular people, which at particular times govern and monopolise their feelings. Sometimes, of course, feelings last only for a moment: a joiner who hits his own thumb with a hammer may swear ferociously for a moment but his bad temper will soon be gone. But the feelings of someone who has been insulted or humiliated or cheated may last for a very long time. They may be so deeply implanted in the victim that they become a part of what we call his or her character: an incident which is deeply felt – which *matters* to a person – may be a critical point in that person's life, a point at which his or her outlook on life in general is subtly but distinctly changed, sometimes for the better, sometimes for the worse. One often hears it said of someone 'He's been a different man since he saw that road accident' or 'She's never been the same since the day she lost her purse.' The rich tapestry of human life is woven out of countless 'minute particulars'.

It is, so to speak, within this tapestry that the church exists and worships. In some places it is close to the centre of the tapestry, in others nearer to a corner: but in all places it is within the tapestry, a part of it. It exists as a living reminder of the sublime truth that 'God was in Christ reconciling the world to himself, not holding their trespasses against them,' and its purpose is the ministry of reconciliation in the place in which it exists, for the sake of the people among whom it exists. To those people many things are happening day by day – things which stir their feelings, whether momentarily or for a long time, whether pleasantly or painfully, whether gladly or angrily: and out of the feelings stirred a person's 'outlook on life' is gradually moulded. It becomes a little closer to, or a little further from, 'what God would have it be' – the God whom Jesus has disclosed to us, the God in whose hands 'all is well: all is very well,' the God who is our friend. The purpose of the ministry of reconciliation is to remind one another of this God not only in public worship but also in private life whenever someone is feeling deeply something which is happening to him or her.

At this point we must consider a second important difference between the world in which Paul exercised his ministry of reconciliation and the world of today. In Paul's day there was among Christians no formal and recognised distinction between what we call today 'clergy' and 'laity'. The seeds of such a distinction were already being sown in Paul's own recognition that in the Christian community different people had different 'gifts' and different contributions to make as members of the 'body of Christ'. But when he occasionally used the Greek word *presbutes* – which is the origin of both of our words 'priest' and 'presbyter' – it is uncertain whether he was referring to a man who had a distinct role or status in the Christian community or simply to an 'old man'. When Paul wrote that 'we' have received both the message and the ministry of reconciliation he was certainly not referring to 'himself and a few others': he was referring to *all* Christians. And still today all Christians are called to be reminders of God – the God who is their friend – to the people among whom they live and work and spend most of their time; to be reminders most especially to people who are going through those critical periods when feelings are strong and deep.

Now this work of 'reminding' does not consist of 'preaching at' people who are going through these crises. It is much less obtrusive than preaching and much more considerate. Often it consists in simply calling on someone and listening quietly to what that person has to say; absorbing, as it were, his or her anxiety or wrath; enhancing his or her joy by allowing it to be expressed. Often it consists of asking for advice or help from someone who is feeling guilt and shame. Sometimes it involves taking the trouble to meet the practical needs of someone at a critical time. Always it requires the integrity of keeping in confidence what is told in confidence. Always it calls for considerateness, tact, sensitivity, understanding of another person's point of view. Always it calls for *grace* in what is said and done. In the ministry of reconciliation we are required not to thrust ourselves or our advice upon others in their times of intense feelings, but rather to make ourselves *available* to them – one might even say to *expose* ourselves to them: and we expose ourselves most effectively when we give to another person our *physical presence*.

Now it is a rather bizarre fact that in current English usage there is no word for the activity of 'giving one's physical presence'. There used to be such a word until about the beginning of this century: it was the word 'assistance'. But in recent times that word has become synonymous with 'help' – with *any* kind of help. I recall an occasion when two French ladies came to attend the Eucharist at a cathedral and asked at the door of the cathedral to which chapel they should go. But their English was not perfect: they made their request using the word 'assistance' in the sense in which it is still used in their own language, saying, 'Where shall we go to assist at the Eucharist?' The man at the door naturally supposed that they wanted to *help* at the Eucharist – to take the collection or sing in the choir or read the Epistle – and courteously explained that all these tasks were already provided for and so he did not see how they *could* assist: whereupon the two young ladies burst into tears saying that they had been told that they could do so and had come all the way from the South of France to do so. I am glad to say that someone who knew French was around to solve the misunderstanding and show the two ladies to their seats. In a sense it was they who were in the right: for the Latin root of the word 'assistance', whether it is used in French or in English, is *adsisto* which means to stand with a person or at a place. The word 'assistance' is a very *physical* word: it denotes putting one's body somewhere, giving one's physical presence to someone. And the gift of one's physical presence is, in a sense, unique: it cannot be wholly or adequately replaced by any other gift or any other means of communication. Neither cards nor telephone calls nor television nor faxes nor the Internet nor anything else in all technology can match the existential power of speaking and listening to another person eye to eye and face to face. In my retirement I sometimes receive visits from old friends. Usually they have told me in advance when they will be coming and I prepare myself for their coming. I call to mind things I want to tell them, mutual friends about whom I want to ask them, bits and pieces that I want to show them and so on. But the moment their faces appear at the door all my agenda go to the wind. Their physical presence has an existential power which is irresistable and cannot be defined. T. S. Eliot once wrote that 'Meeting is for strangers; meeting is for those

who do not know each other'; but, although there is a certain
theoretical wisdom in this, I suspect that when old friends
of his arrived at the door he himself was 'surprised by joy'.
To 'go' to someone at a critical time is as different from
'sending a message' as chalk is different from cheese.

All Christians are called to be ministers of reconciliation
to the people among whom they live. In my young days as
a curate I had the privilege of knowing for a few years a man
called Walter who set an unforgettable example of what such
a minister can do and be. He lived on his own, never married
and never rose higher in social status than to be a labourer
who was sometimes unemployed. He had no particular skills
except on the football field: and it was because the local
church had a football team that as a youth he began to attend
it. He continued to attend it twice every Sunday for the sixty
years until he died. On the football field colleagues were
sometimes quite severely injured, and Walter took to 'going'
to them at their homes to see how they were getting on.
He began to realise how much it meant to the long-term
injured to have someone 'go' to them, and gradually he began
to extend the range of his 'going' to other people in the
neighbourhood. Walter, as I have said, had no particular
skills and was trained in no expertise: he simply made himself
available for anything that, in a difficult time, someone might
need or might want to tell him. I remember that on days
when he was working he would go, *before* he went to work,
to help out of bed a man who had lost a leg in playing
football and another man who was half paralysed: in the
evenings one would see him about the streets every day going
to someone who was ill or whose dog had died or whose
daughter was away on holiday or whose husband had left
her or who could not get to the shops or whose library books

were overdue, or who 'liked a chat'. Once, in a snow storm late on Christmas Eve I almost bumped into Walter getting a bit of shelter in a doorway. I asked him where he was going. 'To So-and-so', he said, 'with a bit of something for Christmas. They haven't much, you know.' I realised when I left him that the doorway in which he was sheltering on Christmas Eve was that of a stable: it seemed extraordinarily appropriate. Walter lived and continued in his ministry for many years after I moved to another parish, but I have heard from friends that he had a heart-attack and dropped dead in the street at the age of seventy seven. A razor and shaving brush were found in his pocket: he way on his way to shave an old man who could not shave himself. I have also been told by friends that over eight hundred people were present in church at Walter's funeral – virtually all of them from that parish.

Clearly Walter was a remarkable man. I knew him only in the early years of his ministry, but even then he seemed to be known by everybody and universally admired and loved. If his name was mentioned in conversation someone would say 'Eh, Walter . . . he's a saint, isn't he?' or 'I call him the Saint of St Thomas.' When Walter retired from his work as a labourer one of the churchwardens immediately retired in order that Walter might be appointed in his place. One might imagine that his universal popularity and influence in the parish could have been somewhat embarrassing to the clergy who succeeded one another in the years of Walter's ministry. But this did not happen: Walter was very clear in his mind that, though his own ministry overlapped with that of the clergy, it was not a substitute for it or an alternative to it. In the very early days of my curacy he explained this to me in some such terms as these: 'I know people like me to go when they need a friend: but sometimes it's more than a friend that they are needing – it's Him. And when you go wearing your collar, it makes them think of Him: but if you *don't* go it makes them feel that He has forgotten them.' So it was that Walter was constantly accosting the vicar or myself and saying, in his staccato way, 'Mrs Smith – 27, Hughes Street – doesn't come to church – you may not know her – I go and I think she's near the end – you'll go won't you?' or 'Fred Brierley – 10 Horace Street – walks with a stick – you'll know him – lost his job – very bitter – I think you should go.'

Years later, in a different parish, Walter's wisdom and insight came home to me. There came to live in the parish a very elderly couple who were both virtually housebound by arthritis. They had no family and no friends near at hand and I did not know of their existence until, one day when I passed, the husband was standing on his crutches at the door. I began to 'go' to them and came to realise that, though they were housebound, they were managing quite well with the help of the social services. They were very appreciative of this help: and one day when I was sitting between them a kind of litany or series of versicles and responses broke out between them. It went something like this:

HE: 'Chiropodist comes to attend to our feet'

SHE: 'Nurse comes to dress my ulcers'

HE: 'Meals-on-wheels come to bring us our dinners'

SHE: 'Man comes from Council to cut our bit of lawn'

HE: 'Social services lady comes to fetch our pension'

SHE: 'Home-help comes twice a week to do our shopping'

HE: 'And she keeps the house clean too'

SHE: 'Doctor comes once a month to see we're all right'

HE: 'And you come to remind us of Him from Whom they all come.'

At the end of the litany I was tempted to say 'Amen'.

The ministry of reconciliation requires of us that we shall 'go' to our neighbours at critical times – give to them our presence – 'assist' them in the old-fashioned sense of that word. In the comparatively recent past this ministry was committed almost exclusively into the hands of the clergy. It was hoped and expected that 'the new vicar would be a good visitor', and in the training of clergy the demands, and the pitfalls, of visiting received a great deal of attention. But in the last thirty years or so the situation has changed. Clergy are fewer per head of population, and lay people are encouraged to take a share in their duties. It has also come about that the social services are undertaking more and more of the tasks which were once left to the clergy; and there is also a more subtle reason why some clergy are inclined to depreciate the importance and significance of visiting. In the early sixties, when this country had got over the Second World War and its consequences, almost every institution in the land decided that it was time 'to take a good hard look at itself' – to identify its purposes, its role in society, and the qualifications and expertise which were necessary in its members and staff for the fulfilment of that role. So far as I know the Church as a whole never set up a commission to take a hard look at itself and identify the qualifications and expertise necessary in its clergy; but many clergy, and groups of clergy, *did* in that period look hard at what they were doing and their qualifications for doing it. They had no problem about what they were doing in church or when they took the sacrament to a devout person who was housebound;

but what were they doing if and when they simply 'went' to a parishioner who was ill or distressed or, at the other extreme, bursting with delight? They had none of the qualifications of a doctor or lawyer or nurse or trained counsellor; they were qualified to preach or pray, but, unless they were asked to – which was unusual – the person to whom they came would be embarrassed or even offended. So it came about that at that period a good many of the younger clergy ceased to be 'good visitors' and put the whole responsibility into the hands of willing lay people. What they did not realise is what Walter told me so succinctly long ago – that priests and ministers are to people in general 'living reminders' of God and if, when God is most needed, they do *not* go – if they withold their 'assistance' – they give the impression to someone that God has forgotten him or her, that he or she does not *matter* to God. 'Going' to people is a *very* important part of the ministry of reconciliation, and clergy who distance themselves from their parishioners, who leave it to lay people 'to do all the visiting' on the grounds that they themselves have 'other things to do', are, as we say nowadays, 'sending the wrong signal altogether' around the parish.

They are also, it seems to me, impoverishing and depriving themselves. At the beginning of this chapter I wrote of the buoyancy of the grace of God and the possibility of 'insulating' oneself from this buoyancy by preoccupation with one's own performance. Clergy are peculiarly susceptible to this possibility. We take our calling and our profession seriously: we feel ourselves directly answerable to God for what we do or fail to do and are prone to anxiety over our own performance – we tend to feel that God is constantly scrutinising that performance and 'counting our trespasses against us'. We fail to relax and allow ourselves to be lifted up and sustained by the grace of God. Yet his grace is ever around us and the closer we keep to our parishioners the more evident that grace becomes. For when we 'go' to people they tell us many stories – stories of events and occasions in their lives which have been important to them and for which, in retrospect, they are very grateful – stories of things which have happened to them in which they recognise, explicitly or by implication, the grace of God. It seems appropriate to bring this chapter to an end with such a story.

A parishioner – I will call her M – happily married and the mother of a little son went into hospital to have her second child. But the baby, a girl, was born with what was then called a hole-in-the-heart, and – whether or not for this reason I do not know – M fell into one of those dreadful post-childbirth depressions. She was kept in hospital for many weeks, and when she was allowed home her husband said that she never smiled and rarely spoke, even to him. When she went out to the shops she did so with a perfectly blank face and spoke only to give her order. When she came to church she sat alone at the back and, lest anyone should speak to her, left a little before the service ended. This went on for months rather than weeks. But one Wednesday morning I met her outside the post-office. Her face looked alive again and I said 'You're looking better, M'. She smiled and said, 'Oh yes, I'm tons better. Haven't I been stupid? I'm ashamed of myself: I don't know how you've all put up with me.' I said 'Never mind that: all that matters is that you are better.' 'Yes,' M said thoughtfully, 'but I'd like to tell you how it happened. It was very strange, Vicar. Last Sunday morning, in church, at twenty past eight, when we were kneeling, I suddenly felt that arms were around me, lifting me up: and as they lifted me up it was as if all the depression fell away from me and I *knew* that everything was all right; and what's more, Vicar, I knew that everything *always will be* all right. It's strange, isn't it?'

For seven years everything was all right. The little girl with the defective heart was doing quite well and the doctors were pleased. But then, one Saturday morning, M's husband went to work to put in a bit of overtime; and at work he fell down dead from a heart attack at the age of 39. I went to M's house in the evening and found a dozen or more of M's and her husband's families who had come to console her. But in fact *she* was consoling *them* – bringing them cups of tea and hugging them. They realised this, and several of them said to me quietly, 'She's in a state of shock, Vicar . . . It hasn't hit her yet . . . She doesn't realise what has happened . . . She'll be different tomorrow.' But she was not in a state of shock. As I was about to leave she took me into the kitchen and said, 'Do you remember what I told you that day outside the post-office?' I nodded, and she went on 'Well, it's still with me, you know: everything's still all right.'

For five years everything remained 'all right'. The little girl's heart condition seemed to be improving and her health was better than it had ever been. But one evening when I called on M she said 'I'm glad you've come. I've got a problem. I've known all along that Judy will *have* to have an operation on her heart some time: and the doctors say that this age – twelve – is the best at which to have it: if it's left much longer it will become more and more risky. But Judy is *so* much better just now – so much enjoying herself – that it seems a shame that she should have to go through a big operation. I don't know what to do – to let the doctors do it or to refuse. What do you think?' I could only say that in a situation like this one was almost *bound* to follow the doctors' advice: and M assented and agreed.

The hospital where the operation had to be done was a long way from home but M had friends who lived near to it, and she and her son went to stay with them until Judy was ready to come home. But something went wrong during the operation and Judy died upon the table.

It was only the day before the funeral that M and her son came home with Judy's body. I called rather late in the evening and M smiled just as ever when she came to the door. 'Would you like to see her?' she said. I said 'Yes, please.' She took me into the front room where the small coffin was placed under the window. She gently moved the linen cloth from Judy's face. We looked down on the child's face, knelt down and said prayers. When we rose M looked down again on Judy's face and said to me, '*Isn't* she lovely, Vicar? *Isn't* she lovely?' Then she carefully replaced the linen cloth, turned to me and said, 'You must have had a long day, Vicar. Will you have a cup of tea?' Neither on that evening nor on any other occasion did M speak one word of bitterness or self-pity or blame. To her 'everything was all right'; or, as Mother Julian put it, 'All is well: all is *very* well.'

It was not long after Judy's death that I moved away from that particular parish but years later, by chance, I met M again. I said 'I'll never forget what you told me that day outside the post-office.' 'Neither will I' she answered with her usual smile: then she added, thoughtfully, 'Of course I didn't realise then what *He* was preparing me for.' She recognised that it was by the grace of God that she had been embraced and sustained in the days of her sorrow.

Chapter Six

THE GOOD MYSTERIES

❦

I HAPPENED TO HEAR recently on the radio part of a phone-in programme. A panel of four professionals – a lawyer, a psychologist and so on – was available in the studio to give advice over domestic and marital problems, and a wife who phoned in explained that her own interests and enthusiasms were drifting so far apart from those of her husband that the marriage was in jeopardy. The first of the professionals to respond to this lady's problem began with the words 'You've only got one life', and each of the other three agreed that this 'hard fact' must be the basis on which they gave their advice. Four professionals were unanimous in broadcasting to millions the 'hard fact' that 'you've only got one life'.

In the public voices of our age, the voices of the media, we very often hear this 'hard fact' asserted – either explicitly or by implication. We are told 'This is the only life that *you* have got: it is *your* life and so you have a right – you owe it to yourself – to get from it all that *you* want, all that gives *you* pleasure, all that *suits* you, all that *satisfies* you, all that *fulfills* you'. This 'philosophy of life' is predominant in a great deal of what we see and hear and read in the media, and its ghastly implications and consequences have recently been brought to light in Cromwell Street, Gloucester, where, for twenty years, two people were satisfying their perverted sexuality by hideous murders of young women.

But my purpose in this chapter is not to point out the dire consequences which may follow from believing that 'you only have one life'. It is to question the truth and validity of that statement – to suggest that the so-called 'hard fact' is no more than an assumption.

Let us remember, first of all, that in the course of human history millions upon millions of people have denied the truth of the statement. Centuries before Christ the philosopher Socrates was telling his young students, from his own experience, that we become, as we grow older, ever more concerned about what awaits us *after* death. Since the time when Jesus dwelt among us Christians have been constantly asserting their belief in the resurrection of the dead and the life of the world to come. In our own day young Muslims are going to their death in holy wars in total confidence that when they die they will be carried immediately to heaven. One might say that until the present century the overwhelming majority of mankind have believed – sometimes with apprehension, sometimes with hope and joy – in the life of the world to come. Until the present century the majority of mankind would have scoffed at people who said 'You have only one life' and thought them very ignorant or naive.

In the present century the tables have been turning. They have not yet turned through 180°: there are still many people who go to their death in quiet hope of the life of the world to come and many who accept the death of someone dear to them with quiet confidence that 'we shall meet again'. Such people still tend to be admired – and even envied – rather than derided. But there is a growing tendency in our society to evade the discussion of death, to condemn it as 'morbid' and to concentrate attention and research on means of prolonging life and deferring death. One hears death referred to as 'obscene': one reads the well-known poem of Dylan Thomas which begins and ends with the words:

> Do not go gentle into that good night;
> Old age should burn and rave at close of day:
> Rage, rage against the dying of the light.

Thomas's words are in stark contrast to those of John Donne who wrote in the sixteenth century:

> Death, be not proud: though some have called thee
> Mighty and dreadful, for thou art not so;
> For those whom thou think'st thou dost overthrow
> Die not, poor Death; nor yet canst thou kill me . . .
> One short sleep past, we wake eternally
> And Death shall be no more: Death, *thou* shalt die!

Thomas's attitude to death was very different, too, from that of St Francis who referred to 'thou most kind and gentle death, waiting to hush our latest breath,' and from that of Tennyson who, in the middle of the last century, addressed to God the confident words:

> Thou wilt not leave us in the dust:
> Thou madest man, he knows not why;
> He thinks he was not made to die;
> And Thou hast made him: thou art just.

And I would add to these testimonies to a more positive attitude to death than that of Thomas the words which I first encountered on a tombstone beside the ruins of a priory on the island of Oronsay in the Hebrides. I discovered later that they were a quotation from a poem of Edmund Spencer, beautifully inscribed in the script and spelling of the eighteenth century; and I read, 'Sleep after toyle, port after stormy seas, ease after warre, death after life doth greatly please.'

So the question arises, 'Why is it that in the present century and in our society, the general attitude to death is becoming less positive than it was among our forebears?' – 'Why is it that we spend so much of our endeavours in deferring death and so little in preparing ourselves for death?' To say that this change in our attitude to death is due to 'the decline of religion' would be, of course, to beg the question: for the essence of all religions is our relationship with an Other which transcends the years, whether few or many, in which we 'live and move and have our being' in *this* world. To say that the decline of religion *accounts for* the belief that 'you only live once' would be absurd – for it actually *is* that belief. What we must consider is why this belief has become so widespread – at least in the Western world – during the present century.

The first reason – in time though not in importance – has been the impact and influence of Marxism. One might say that it is a political reason. Marx was both an advocate and a prophet of a radical change – a revolution – which lay ahead in the relationship between capital and labour, between those who owned the means of production and those who operated and laboured at the means of production. He foresaw the day when the labouring masses – over-worked and poorly paid – would rebel and take over the machinery of production from the relatively few capitalists who were its present owners and beneficiaries. Marx believed that this revolution – this rising of the masses against their relatively few exploiters – was bound to come, and that its coming was delayed only by the passivity, the inertia, of the masses; and he attributed this inertia, at least in part, to their religion. He spoke of religion as 'the opium of the people' – the drug, as it were, which consoled the masses in their present misery by hope and expectation of a better life in the world to come. He considered religion an obstacle to the revolution which he both advocated and foresaw.

In the course of this century the revolution has both come and gone in many nations, and in the last decade or so Marxism has lost a good deal of its appeal and influence in the world at large. But it retains its influence upon religion, and, in particular, upon the Christian religion. It draws our attention to *this* world – to the way the world around us actually *is*; it suggests that to indulge in thoughts of 'the life of the world to come' is to console ourselves with 'opium': it calls on us to be very *active* in remedying injustice and abolishing poverty and improving in general the world in which we find ourselves. One might almost say that Marx replaced St Paul's words 'set your affection on things above, not on things on the earth' with his own version: 'set your affection on things on the earth, not on things above'. Certainly many Christians of this century have been inclined, under the influence of Marxism, to devote their thoughts and energies to the improvement of this world rather than to reflection and meditation on the life of the world to come: and some have identified themselves publicly as 'Christian Marxists' or 'Marxist Christians'.

But much more important in this century than the influence of Marxism has been the advance of scientific knowledge and its remarkable achievements – achievements which for the most part have been beneficial to mankind. To the man in the street the advance has been awesome in its range and the achievements have been evident in daily life. Every day, by their tests and experiments and studies of statistics, scientists are coming to know what was not known before and to achieve what was not possible before. Achievements prove and display the validity of scientific investigation, the truth – that is to say the trustworthiness – of what scientists report and say. In previous centuries people were inclined to accept as trustworthy whatever was written in a very old book or whatever had been handed down from generation to generation from time immemorial or whatever was told them by a wise old man or woman. It was to the past that in previous centuries people looked for truth: now it is to scientists. It follows that we tend to be sceptical about any claim or any statement which has not been validated by the investigations of scientists: and it is undoubtedly this scepticism which accounts for the decline of religion in this century and the unanimous agreement of four professionals to the 'hard fact' that 'you have only one life'. Wide as is the range of scientific investigation we cannot expect it to extend to 'the life of the world to come'. It is true, of course, that scientists are occasionally persuaded to investigate what we call 'paranormal phenomena' – 'happenings' or 'appearances' which seem to imply that someone who has died is still living somewhere and the physical presence of this person is still detectable at certain times and at certain places in this world. But the investigation always comes to nothing: for it is only the normalities of this world that are detectable and explicable by scientific methods, and if anything is 'paranormal' it is by definition excluded from effective scientific investigation. Our tendency to doubt the truth of any claim or statement which has not been validated by scientific investigation is not only widespread: it is also natural.

But this, of course, does not mean that scientists as such tell us that 'you have only one life' or that all scientists are lying if and when they say, 'we look for the resurrection of the dead and the life of the world to come'. Far from it. Scientists are human beings before they are scientists. They acquire, each in his or her particular discipline, a degree and depth of knowledge which is lacking in many of us and, in the present century, awesome to most of us; and their discipline requires that new knowledge which they report or publish shall be validated by tests, experiments and statistical studies. Knowledge so validated proves to be reliable, trustworthy, true: it is beneficial to mankind and almost universally respected. But the mind of a scientist is not monopolised by truth which he or she has validated, nor yet by the the sum total of truth which scientists have accumulated. It is not by tests or experiments that a scientist knows that he is tired or that she loves her fiancé or that the children are being naughty or that the traffic is moving slowly. A scientist has as many things on his or her mind as has any other person; and that mind, though it may extend its range to the awesome extremities of space or be focused upon the behaviour of particles of matter unimaginably minute, is inclined to become, when it reaches these extremities, a little *tentative* in its conclusions. In the publisher's cover to the autobiography of Sir Bernard Lovell, the creator and director of the great radio-telescopes at Jodrell Bank, we read these words: 'Before revolutionary and entrepreneurial work such as that of Bernard Lovell was carried out, it was arrogantly believed that only science could explain the universe. This assumption has passed away with the realisation that the search for solutions uncovers even deeper mysteries.' Towards the end of his book Lovell himself quotes with approval the words of another distinguished scientist to the effect that we can make sense of our relationship with our fellow men and with the universe 'only in terms of a God – partly seen in science, and in art and history and philosophy, partly experienced in wholly personal terms'. To put the problem crudely: it is generally accepted by contemporary scientists that the universe came into being approximately fifteen billion years ago; that at that point, which was the beginning of time, all the matter of which the universe consists was compacted at one infinitesimal spot which was the beginning of space; that fifteen billion years ago the compacted matter exploded from that spot and time began to flow and space began the expansion which continues to the present day. This 'big-bang theory' of the origin of the universe has been validated by the detection within the universe of certain radio waves which, according to the laws of nature, can *only* have been generated by an explosion of such magnitude at the beginning of time; and only a rash or foolish person would fail to accept the conclusion to which scientists have come or to admire the skill and patience with which they have reached it.

But it is not rash or foolish to be a little bemused by the scientists' conclusion, and no doubt some scientists are themselves bemused. Science advances by identifying the causes of things that are and the reasons why things happen; but in their investigation of the origin of the universe scientists come up against compacted matter which has no cause and an explosion of that matter for which there is no reason. It is as if at this point science comes to a dead end or a blank wall and to the man in the street who asks, not unreasonably, where the compacted matter came from, the scientist can only reply 'from nowhere because as yet there was no space', and to anyone who uses the phrase 'before the big bang' the scientist must object on the grounds that there was no 'before' because time had not yet begun. To the man in the street the scientists' 'explanations' are not very helpful.

Now in one brief and memorable sentence the great philosopher of this century, Ludwig Wittgenstein, identified, as it were, the blank wall beyond which science can go no further. Referring to 'the world' – by which, of course he meant what we should call 'the universe' – Wittgenstein wrote 'Not *how* the world is is the mystery but *that* it is.' *How* the world is – one might even say 'how the world *works*' – is the concern of scientists and the field of their investigations and discoveries, but *that* the world is – that the universe exists – is mystery. The word 'mystery' is derived from the Greek word *muein* which means 'to keep one's mouth shut': a mystery is something which one knows but cannot express in words. We know that the universe exists, and scientists tell us more and more about how it works, but *that* it exists is a fact so amazing, so awesome, that we cannot express it in words. Wittgenstein told a friend of occasions when he looked at some particular thing which existed – his own hand, for instance. He looked at it very intensely; was fascinated by it; found it more and more remarkable that his hand should exist; felt it more and more wonderful that *anything* should exist; felt himself awestruck by the miracle of existence. Wonder at the mystery of existence is not confined to Wittgenstein. There is a classic description of it in Dostoevsky's novel *The Possessed*. The student Kirillov tries to explain to Stavrogin the effect on him of looking at 'a leaf from a tree'. 'I saw a yellow one lately', Kirillov says, 'It was a little green. It was decayed at the edges. It was blown by the wind.' 'What's that?' asks Stavrogin, 'An allegory?' 'No,' Kirillov answers, 'I'm not speaking of an allegory but of a leaf, only a leaf.' Even something so familiar as one's own hand or so common as a decaying leaf can evoke wonder at its existence. How things work in the world, how they cause, and are caused by, other things, is the concern of scientists, but that they *exist* in the world, that there *is* a world for them to exist *in*, is a fact beyond the capacity of science to explain, a mystery which even scientists are unable to express in words.

But the mystery which cannot be expressed in words can be *felt*, and felt not only by exceptional people like Wittgenstein and Dostoevsky. I suspect that most of us have occasional experiences of wonder – experiences evoked most frequently by things and sounds of exceptional beauty but sometimes evoked by looking intensely at some quite ordinary thing such as one's own hand or a leaf from a tree or water coming from a tap or the body of a tiny insect or the pen with which one writes; and one might say that this wonder is the theme and the inspiration of many poets such as Wordsworth and Coleridge and William Blake. And there is a further point to be made about the experience of wonder: it brings with it a kind of combination of security and joy. Dostoevsky's Kirillov continues his conversation with Stavrogin in almost ecstatic terms: 'the leaf is good', he says, 'everything's good.' 'Everything?' asks Stavrogin. Kirillov replies, 'Everything. Man is unhappy because he doesn't know he's happy. It's only that. That's all, that's all. If anyone finds out, he'll become happy at once, that minute. It's all good. I discovered it all of a sudden.' Kirillov is, to put it mildly, eccentric; but his creator, Dostoevsky, had a profound insight into the depths of human nature and human experience, and Wittgenstein, the most influential philosopher of our century, spoke of the assurance that *all is well* which came to him as he wondered at the existence of his own hand. To wonder at the mystery of existence, to wonder that anything at all exists, is to receive a welcome assurance, a sense of security which brings with it gladness and joy. In this wonder we become aware of a truth which does not depend on scientific discovery of 'how the world works'.

And we become aware in another way of truth which transcends scientific investigation and discovery. Each human being knows that he or she exists. How human beings have evolved from more primitive creatures is discovered by the sciences of anthropology and palaeontology, and the progress of the human foetus from conception to birth is known to, and watched over by, geneticists, paediatricians and other scientists of the medical profession. *How* it happens that a particular person is male or female, blue-eyed or hazel-eyed, fair-haired or dark-haired, is known to scientists in ever increasing detail and with ever increasing clarity. But what is not known, and cannot be known, by scientists is *who* I am, 'what it is like to be me'. That I am who I am is known only to me. I am aware of myself as being myself and not being someone else. I may imagine that I am someone else, or wish that I were someone else, but I know that I am *only* imagining or wishing. I may wish in some circumstances that I were *anyone but* myself, but again I know that I am *only* wishing. I may pretend to be someone else, but though my pretence may delude other people I know that it is *only* pretence. That I am who I am is for me the hardest of all hard facts, and my awareness of it is beyond the power of scientific studies to explain or even to investigate. Within the mystery of existence – the mystery that anything at all exists – lies the mystery that I am I and you, dear reader, are you. That I am I and you are you is a mystery within a mystery.

A mystery is something which is known to be true but which cannot be expressed in words. As we have seen, the root-meaning of 'mystery' is 'keeping one's mouth shut', and certainly no scientific statements or mathematical formulae can convey the whole truth of a mystery. But poets worthy of the name refuse 'to keep their mouths shut', and so do writers of love letters or letters of condolence (how many such letters begin with 'I can't tell you how much . . .' and then go on to tell!); and I suspect that many artists and musicians, though their mouths are shut, are aspiring to convey in their own medium truth which is wrapped in mystery. Here we must consider the word 'meaning': for my awareness of who I am includes an awareness of the underlying meaning to me of certain people, certain events, even of certain things. I know, of course, that I am affected if the light in my room goes out suddenly or my pen runs dry or a tooth begins to ache: I know that it is to me and not to someone else that these misfortunes have occurred. But I am also affected by the meaning to me of another person or an event or a thing. The philosophy of reductionism which has recently been in vogue in some quarters seems to me to imply that 'nothing means anything': if this is so, that philosophy is mere folly. I know, as surely as I know that I exist, that certain people, events and things affect who I am by what can only be described as their *meanings* to me – meanings which vary in their depths or powers or intensities. It is the power of meaning which makes possible all human relationships. It constrains me to treat one person in one way and a

different person in a different way. I am constrained to behave
to a person who 'means a great deal to me' in a different way
from that in which I behave to a person who means little or
nothing to me; I am aware of *owing* to the one what I do
not owe to the other. The word 'constrained' is more appropriate than 'compelled': for, such is the mystery of my
awareness of who I am, that I can feel that it is by my own
choice that – at Christmas for example – I send to a person
who means a great deal to me a costly present and to one who
means less only a simple card. The choice is certainly my
choice: it is not the choice of anyone else. But it is made
under the pressure of the meanings to me of the two people
involved.

It is the power of meaning which not only makes human
relationships possible but also accounts for our *interest* in the
world we live in and the things that it contains. The disease
or defect commonly called 'autism' might be described as a
condition in which nothing means anything to the patient.
He or she is aware of the world but has no interest in it. I
remember visiting in hospital a young man who was in this
sad condition. He was sitting alone in the day room: and
when the door opened and the nurse and I came in he did
not look up. I had brought a basket of fruit for him, but
when I gave it to him he made no response but left it lying
in his lap. I gave him a message from his mother, told him
various things, asked him questions, but there was no
response nor any change in his face. But he was not insen-
sible, for twice he spoke – slowly, in a low, flat voice. He
said, 'Your coat is wet', and a little later, 'The window is
dirty.' In both cases what he said was true. He was aware of
the world but it meant nothing to him, it did not interest
him. He came home a few days later and killed himself by

hiding behind a wall and throwing himself, laughing, under the front wheels of the first heavy lorry that came along the road. The world did not interest him: it had no meaning for him.

For most of us the world *is* interesting: all sorts of people and events and things *mean* something to us. We know that they do so, but rarely if ever can we define in words how or why they do so. I know that I enjoy listening to one piece of music rather than another, that I admire and trust one person more than another, that I am more interested in one sport or game than another, that I prefer one kind of food or drink to another; and I cannot deny these hard facts. But I cannot explain them or account for them except in the vaguest of terms – in words which, in effect, beg the question. If I am engrossed in a particular book and asked why I am reading it, my reply that 'I find it interesting' begs the question. I know, and cannot deny, that the world of people and events and things interests me, has power of meaning for me. That it does so has made possible the birth of science and its remarkable development in recent years. If I were not I and you were not you and everyone were not who he or she is, there would be no human relationships and also no scientific investigations and discoveries. So, as we have seen, within the mystery of *existence* – the mystery of the fact that anything at all exists – lies what we might call the mystery of *identity* – the mystery of the fact that I am I and you are you; and now we see that there is also a third level or depth of mystery – the mystery of *meaning* – the mystery of the fact that the world of people and events and things *means* something to me and to you and to the great majority of human beings. We know these facts to be true – true but inexplicable – *mysteries*.

The purpose of this chapter is to question the statement 'you only live once' and to suggest that, so far from being a 'hard fact', it is no more than a rather fragile assumption. Of course our *bodies* only live once. But I am not *just* my body, nor are you *just* your body. A biography is much more than a history of someone's body – a detailed medical history of gains and losses in weight and rises and falls in blood pressure and so on: and if someone were to lose both legs in an accident we should not refer to him or her as 'part of Mr X,' or 'most of Miss Y'. Each of the two would retain the same identity and remain to all of us the same person. Clearly 'I' am more than 'my body' and 'you' are more than 'your body'; and what each of us has or is, in addition to a body, is an 'identity' or 'individuality' or, as some would say, a 'personhood'.

Now our forbears did not use any one of these three rather clumsy words to denote what I have or am in addition to a body. Instead of a many-syllabled word they used a word of only one syllable – the word 'soul'. For them 'body and soul' went together as naturally as 'knife and fork' go together to us. 'To keep body and soul together' meant to them 'to keep someone alive'; to express support for an endeavour or an opinion one said 'I'm with you body and soul'. Colloquially, a person was sometimes referred to simply as 'a body' – 'he's a busy-body' 'she's a funny little body' – but such a reference was either jocular or faintly derogatory: whereas to speak of a person as simply 'a soul' – 'a good soul', 'a brave soul', 'a kind soul' or 'a poor soul' – was to express a degree of admiration or sympathy for a person. One might say that by our forbears, for whom 'body and soul' naturally went together, 'soul' was respected rather more than 'body'.

It is quite recently, within my own lifetime, that the word

'soul' has drifted out of common and colloquial usage. Its use is confined to strictly and specifically religious gatherings and occasions. The reason for this is not difficult to see. For ages before the science of biology began to develop, religion – at least the Christian religion – taught that the soul was *inside the body*, that it was a part of the *matter* of the body – a rather misty kind of matter which, on the death of the body, departed from the body and floated away to its destiny elsewhere – whether in heaven or in hell. Now in the ages before anaesthetics came into use only *dead* bodies could be dissected and studied – bodies from which it was believed that the soul had already departed: so medical and biological knowledge, such as it was, could not challenge religious teaching, and painters and sculptors could depict the misty soul actually drifting away from the dead body. But when the development of anaesthetics enabled surgeons and bio-logists to investigate the interior of *living* bodies they found there no matter which could be identified as 'the soul'. This scientific discovery gradually became common knowledge. I remember from my boyhood an occasion when a young doctor, fresh from his studies, told me earnestly and emphati-cally that souls do not exist, that there is no such thing as a soul, that he had no soul and neither had I. Science denied what religion taught; science dismissed as a non-entity 'the soul' which was constantly being referred to in religious teaching and practice. Religious teaching was misleading and even fraudulent in telling us that we have a soul. Surely the conviction, or at least suspicion, that religion is fraudulent in this respect is the cause not only of the drift of the word 'soul' out of common usage but also of what we call 'the decline of religion' in the present century.

But still we live – all of us – surrounded and enfolded by

mystery: mystery which cannot be denied but also cannot be explained or clarified in words. Wittgenstein used few and simple words to point to, to draw attention to, mystery – 'the mystery is not *how* the world is but *that* it is'. Scientists investigate and discover *how* the world works; they discover how long it has existed and the laws of nature which govern and order it; but that it exists – that anything at all exists – is a mystery which cannot be denied but which also cannot be explained by scientists. Wittgenstein also spoke privately of his own *wonder* as he looked hard at some particular thing which existed, and in his wonder felt a certain gladness and security. I think that *wonder* at something that exists brings to many of us a childlike delight and confidence that 'all is well'; when we wonder at the mystery of existence it presents itself to us not as a nightmare or a threat but as a good mystery, a welcome mystery.

Within the mystery of existence lies the mystery of what I have called so far 'my identity' – my awareness that I am I and your awareness that you are you. From now on I shall refer to that mysterious awareness not as 'my identity' but as 'my soul': for, as we have seen, it is common knowledge now that my soul, unlike my heart and my pancreas, is not a part of the interior of my body. In the past religion was mistaken in teaching that it is. We should recognise and admit this error. We should admit that the soul is not *in* the body; but we can still speak of 'body *and* soul' as our forbears did. My soul is what I have, or am, *in addition* to my body', and it would be an improvement to our language if we all spoke of this addition as 'my soul' rather than 'my identity' 'my individuality', 'my uniqueness' or 'my personhood'.

Each one of us knows his or her own soul as no one else knows it. I can write with authority only about my own soul:

from what other people write or tell me I sometimes gain an impression of other souls, but it is only a vague impression and may be a quite wrong impression. Speaking only for myself I can say that only when I am asleep am I unaware of my soul – and unaware of my body also. When I am awake I am sometimes aware of a kind of tension, or even conflict, between my body and my soul. For instance, my foot or my tooth is painful and my soul is affected by the pain. The pain urges, motivates, me to take some tablets or go to the doctor; but my soul may declare that the pain is bearable or will soon be gone. Sometimes I am scarcely aware of my body; it stands or turns or walks almost instinctively and I am, so to speak, alone with my soul. I am thinking about something – my brain is busy in my head and medical science could tell me a good deal about brain cells and their performance which are involved in my thinking. But only my soul experiences and evaluates what I am thinking – whether it is pleasant or depressing to think about it, whether it is worth thinking about, whether my thoughts are fair or unfair, clear or muddled and so on. My soul thinks about my own thinking. There is no limit to the depths to which what we call introspection can go. My soul is my mystery, and your soul, dear reader, is yours; and my mystery is my privilege and your mystery is your privilege; and that privilege is the only safe and sure ground of what we call nowadays self-esteem.

The third mystery which we have detected is the mystery of *meaning*. The sad and tragic condition called autism makes us aware of what existence would be like if nothing in the world meant anything to us; and the parents of children who are so afflicted are worthy not only of our sympathy but of all possible endeavours by the medical profession to detect the cause of autism and find means of alleviation and cure. To Wittgenstein's memorable words that 'the mystery is not *how* the world is but *that* it is . . .' we should add the words 'and *that* it has meaning for us'. We know, and cannot deny, the power of meaning; but *why* it is, how it comes about, that certain people and events and things 'mean so much' to some of us and so little to others is a question which has not yet been investigated by scientists and perhaps never will be. All we know is that the world interests us, has meaning for us; and we are glad and grateful that it does so. The mystery of meaning is a *gracious* mystery.

Now how does all this bear upon our thinking about death – death which, when we are old, so frequently takes from us a beloved member of the family or a well-known neighbour or an old and dear friend and reminds us forcibly that the day of our own death cannot be very far away? For some of my readers there will be no problem: their robust faith in the God revealed to us in Jesus Christ will 'take the sting' from death and enable them to 'look for the life of the world to come' with eager hope and unfailing confidence: they will be wholly assured of reunion in the world to come with all those whom they have loved in this world and, in St Paul's words, that 'they will know even as they themselves are known'. There will will be others whose assent to this same faith will be genuine but a little fragile: what their souls believe may be disturbed by their feelings or their intellect. Their feelings of guilt – their awareness of sin unknown to others – may introduce an element of fear into their expectations of the life of the world to come; though believing that, in St Paul's words, 'God does not hold our trespasses against us', they cannot help feeling and fearing that they themselves may be exceptions to that general truth. Others of us have intellectual difficulties when we ponder on 'the life of the world to come'. We find it inconceivable that there could be *life* when the body is reduced to dust and ashes; we cannot even imagine what that life would be, and the images of heaven which appear in the Scriptures and in hymns seem to us naive and childish.

When these intellectual doubts assail me I turn my mind to the mysteries which enfold me. They are inexplicable, inconceivable, unimaginable and yet undeniable – the mystery of existence, the mystery of my soul, the mystery of meaning. I find them unthreatening mysteries, welcome mysteries, good mysteries. By comparison with the mysteries the death of my body is a rather unimportant event, and I am inclined to echo John Donne's words 'Death, be not proud, though some have called thee mighty and terrible: for thou art not so'. There is a reality which so transcends and enfolds the dying of my body and its return to dust and ashes that the statement that 'you only live once' is not even an assumption: it is a gross presumption. And the name of that reality is God; and the grace of God has been disclosed to mankind in Jesus Christ.

So, dear reader, 'Fare well in Christ'. I offer to you a poem which I wrote, so to speak, to myself some twenty years ago when, being ill, I thought it unlikely that I should ever work again:

Joseph of Arimathaea's Easter

'He's gone,' says Joseph, and, with Pilate's leave
Eases the nails and lowers him from the Tree,
Wraps him in reverent and tender thoughts
And lays him in the cave called Memory.

––––––

That cave is deeply hewn in Joseph's heart:
All that's within will always be his own:
In memory's cave the treasure of his past
Is safe for ever, walled and sealed by stone.

'He's safe', says Joseph, 'safe in this cool place
And no one now can take my Lord away.
In years to come I'll still see his dear face
As clearly as I've seen it on this day.'

'He's gone!' cries Joseph at the empty tomb:
But Mary says, 'He's left a word for you:
He cannot rest content to be your past,
So he has risen to be your future too.'